Leaving the Faith

# of Our Fathers

By Lois Requist

Leaving the Faith or our Fathers
By Lois Requist
All Rights Reserved
Copyright 2025
Independently Published
www.loisrequist.com

ISBN: 979-8-9958786-0-5

Editors: Mary Eichbauer, Linda Hastings, Tamar Enoch
Cover Art: Samantha McNally
Cover Design: Carrie Requist
Reviews: Anne Grodin, Lois Kazakoff, Gayle Vasser, James White
Interior Layout: Carrie Requist
Publishing Assistance: Carrie Requist, Tony Requist

Also by Lois Requist

Where Lilacs Bloom
First Edition, 2000, Second Edition, 2017

RVING SOLO ACROSS AMERICA
...without a cat, dog, man, or gun

Late Harvest Green
An Idaho Farm Family Through the 20th Century

Prologue

I was eleven the night I pulled my sin-ridden body toward the altar to beg for God's forgiveness and mercy.

While the choir hummed, "Just as I am without one plea, but that thy blood was shed for me," the preacher, his voice, earlier calm and measured, now ramped it up to an emotional high.

"If you don't get saved tonight, you might be killed in an automobile accident on the way home. Then, you'll burn in hell forever. Your mother will look down from heaven, and see your flesh burning, but she will feel no compassion or sadness for you. There's only happiness in heaven. Do you want to take that chance? Come to Jesus tonight! Know the joy of loving the Lord! Or burn in hell forever!"

Even then, I couldn't quite picture my mother happily sitting on a cloud in heaven, not giving a thought to her daughter roasting in hell.

We attended the Northwest Nazarene Church in Nampa, Idaho for the first years of my life. That included Sunday morning and evening services, Wednesday night prayer meetings, and sometimes special services. The summer tent revival—when all five of the Nazarene churches in town joined together and brought in well-known evangelists to preach—was a highlight.

That warm summer evening in 1950 began with a family picnic. Then it was on to the revival. My four siblings and I looked forward to the meeting because the crowds were large, we could slip away from the service, run with other kids, peek in the backs of cars where teenagers were making out, startle the neckers, and run away laughing. This and the thrill of escaping the oft-repeated story of sin and redemption, these were our delights. We could still hear the service going on in the background.

As children, if we tried to explain what we'd been taught in church, we always reduced everything to the lowest common denominator. In the parlance of my peers, churches were rated on how much freedom they allowed. It went like this: Catholics can do anything—stay out all night, mess around, whatever. The next day, they go to confession, say what they did, buy a candle, and are forgiven. Some Protestant churches were what we called, "Once in grace, always in grace," churches. Confess your sins and ask for forgiveness once. You were pretty well covered. But in our church, you could sin in word, thought, or deed at any time and, when you did, you were headed for Hell.

I guess I was born into the wrong family!

These were the only churches I knew. By the time I was twelve, we started attending another church, which taught us about a "kingdom" message, later known by various names, such as the Christian Identity Movement, which believes that White Europeans who settled America were the lost ten tribes of Israel, destined to settle this land and start a nation. The Jewish Conspiracy—the moneylenders—were the Synagogue of Satan. They controlled much of health care, education, entertainment, banks, the government, so we could not put our faith in any of those establishments.

At that time, I was fine with all that. What did I know? Nothing at all about any faiths other than Christian ones. My mother presented these ideas in a benevolent fashion. We were to be a servant nation to bring the world to the Christian God. Heaven would be on Earth.

When I moved away from home, talked to people with different beliefs, read books, thought about it all, I began to question these beliefs. Belief in the Bible or God is based on faith, not fact. Did I have that faith?

I would never have written this book except for political events in recent years. I remember the anxiety spreading through me when I heard protesters in Charlottesville, Virginia, in August 2017 say, "Jews will not replace us!"

I'd always thought that the beliefs of the Kingdom message, which I learned as a young person, were held by a tiny number of people, so small as to be inconsequential. With the Charlottesville protest and the January 6th attempt to take over the U.S. government by many who proclaimed themselves to be White Supremacists, I was jarred to realize how wrong I'd been, and the terrible consequences possible when one race and one religion holds itself to be "the one and only" and wants that to be the law of the land. This land. Think of the Taliban, of all countries where politics and religion are one and the same. Think Afghanistan, where women are forced to wear outfits that cover them completely and aren't allowed to go to school.

I felt I had to share the stories I'd written over many years. Poems and stories in which what I believe changes as time and experience has impacted me. The faith I have now is based in my own experiences. That brings me fulfillment and joy. I don't have to worry if what I'm reading, writing, or experiencing is contrary to any religion.

Chapter One

Reflections on Early Childhood

Mother had her hands full when I was born in 1939. I was the fourth of four children within four years. No automatic washing machine or dryer, no diaper service, no indoor bathroom served to make her job easier. Nor did my father, who was 24 years older than she was and had no idea how, or desire to, care for his children. My oldest sister, Ernestine, has a baby book filled with notations about when she first smiled, rolled over, crawled, sat up, walked, or did any of the things children do at some point. My name and birth date—that's it, in my book. Mother was simply too busy by then to write down such trivialities. Still, she managed, as she always did.

What I remember from those early years is vague. It includes the stories that were repeated and the things I recall. I began writing down what I remembered 40 or 50 years ago, so now those early stories are fixed in me as facts. Mother used to say that I loved to eat. She would take me from the table when I was two so I would stop eating.

My earliest memories don't include Father. He wasn't there. We lived on Karcher Road in a small house on five acres, on the outskirts of Nampa, Idaho. When World War II broke out, my father, too old to go into the army, went several hundred miles away to Hanford, Washington, where he worked in an atomic defense plant. My sister, Ernestine, and two brothers, Harry and Stanley, walked the mile or so to the closest school. I stayed at home with my mother. I was rarely alone with her the rest of our lives.

When I was about four, a huge tire came off a truck and headed towards the window where I was sitting, interrupted at the last minute by a telephone pole, so the wheel rolled harmlessly to one side and settled in a ditch.

"Could have killed you," Mother said as we stood looking down at the still steaming tire. "God was watching out for you. If it had hit the window just right, it coulda' killed you."

Mother was watching out for me and so was God! How splendid.

Besides caring for us, Mother raised goats, those animals that roamed about the land eating anything they could get their mouths around. People rented them to eat their weeds and junk.

In this rural setting, every spring, farmers plowed the nearby fields. They worked with the seasons, planting in spring, irrigating the crops through the summer until harvest time, which demanded their full attention. The fruits of their labor were their livelihood. Nothing was taken for granted.

The morning sun came in through the east windows. Children went to school. People went to church and to the store when necessary. Our habits were about as regular as those of nature.

Grandfather came out from his home in Nampa often to help my mother—his daughter—with the work. He was a large man with a thick, full beard. Though kind, he was a little daunting to me.

He lived in town with his second wife, whom we called Grandma. Our biological grandmother died when Mother was fourteen. Mother often said about my step-grandmother, "She's not your real Grandma." The two of them got along, as far as I know, but Mother didn't want her mother forgotten.

******

I wrote this story so many years ago. It was probably the first one I wrote about my childhood.

One morning in 1945, Mother was ironing while I sat on a stool talking to her. The radio played in the background. Something the announcer said caught Mother's ear. She set the iron down, turned in her faded cotton housedress—a material I still associate with comfort—and rotated the dial. The voice became louder.

"President Roosevelt is dead," the voice said.

"Oh-h, oh, my…" Mother said, staring out the window.

The radio repeated the words and something about Georgia.

This moment lingers, a glass shattering, as if I knew things were going to change. Or did I invent that all later? Pictures come before me. The war ended. Father came home. The house that was warm, light, and pale yellow—a safe place—disappeared, replaced by another house painted gray. I see broken pieces of dark colors. What is the color of anger?

Mother turned slowly back to the iron, absently reaching down, unplugging the cord, and setting the iron on its end.

"Come," she said, "We'll go over to Mrs. Taggert's house." She smoothed my dark brown hair a little with her warm hand and helped me on with a sweater. Then she brushed her hair a bit and pulled on a jacket. We went to the Taggerts's back door, as was customary for such unplanned visits. The front door was for formal occasions.

Mrs. Taggert greeted Mother as if she had been expecting us and patted me on the head.

"You must have heard the news. Amazing!"

"Yes, isn't it! Just had to talk to somebody," Mother said. "Wonder what this will do to the war."

"And, that Mr. Truman. S'pose he knows what to do? Well, sit down. I'll put on some coffee."

Coffee was a generous offer. It was rationed, as was sugar and gasoline.

Soon after school started in September, I came here with Mother for the first time. Mrs. Taggert had invited us over and led us to the living room. It was a marvel to me, the pretty, untouched room with soft furniture in quiet tones, highly polished wooden tables, dishes, and glass objects in various shapes and colors. At our house, nothing was unused or bought just to look at. We didn't have a room mostly there just to be pretty. Mother held on to my hand and told me not to touch anything, which made me want to even more. I loved to watch a certain tall glass vase catch the light, hold it, or send it on in a different hue and a new direction.

On this occasion, while the coffee perked, Mrs. Taggert poured a glass of milk for me and cut a piece of white cake for each of us.

"Cream or sugar?"

When the coffee was ready, she poured the dark steaming liquid into two cups and handed one to Mother across the formica table. She looked around for a moment, and satisfied that we had everything, sat down, stirred sugar into her coffee, and took a sip.

I liked sitting with the women while they discussed things I knew nothing about. It was so grown-up and did not happen when my sister and brothers were home. I looked all around the room, ate the cake, and wished for more, but knew better than to ask.

"What do you hear from your husband in Hanford?" Mrs. Taggert asked.

"Well, it sounds like they work long hours. Still the money is good. He lives in a trailer house with some other folks."

"I wonder what will happen now."

"With the President dying? I don't know. Four kids, the animals, and the place to tend. I don't have much time to think about it. I do wonder, though, how it will all turn out, and when the war will be over. Then, my husband will come home."

"Oh, I'm sure you'll be glad when that happens."

"Yes, of course. Do you suppose…"

The women took the news, worked it over as they would knead bread dough, adding a little flour, pressing their knuckles into the white mass, turning, and shaping it into a workable whole.

They did not dismiss me that morning, as they did sometimes.

"Go and play, dear," Mother would say on such occasions, turning to the neighbor, "Little pitchers have big ears."

When encouraged to go away, I would wander towards the books or toys, with one ear to what they were saying. Adult conversation was best when it was not supposed to be heard. What they wanted us to hear—the admonitions, rules, and directions to follow—were said clearly, repeatedly.

This morning, however, the subject was not gossip, but rather large and grand, so I was left to listen until Mother said, "Well, we better be going. Lots to do."

She took my hand. We said goodbye and crossed the road to our home.

******

Many years later, a grandmother myself, I reflected on my mother and those long-ago experiences.

January 2000. Driving on the freeway toward Oakland, going to take care of Melissa, my granddaughter, on Martin Luther King's Birthday, I listen to the radio. The morning is gray. On KGO, the announcer, Ted Wygant, hears from a listener who says it is raining hard in Livermore. The weather report isn't quite doing it. I need something more uplifting. Pushing buttons, I find the CD of spirituals and gospels.

While I drive into the Caldecott Tunnel, a voice, low, full, and sad, sings, "Nobody knows the trouble I've seen," taking the "Nobody," real slow, like a dozen o's were there, all coming from deep inside, needing expression.

Here I am, sixty years old, and gospel music, the songs I grew up with, still touch me profoundly. "Amazing Grace" loosens my whole body, sending my psyche into a kind of free rise.

Music of many kinds reaches me. If I could sing, I wouldn't be writing. I can do without the sermons, but the hymns, I'll come back for those. Someone told me that the music, "goes right to your soul," and I like that idea, though I don't know about that soul business anymore.

What is the truth? Do we have a soul? I wonder.

My granddaughter and her parents, and now the new baby twins, live in Alameda, necessitating a drive through Oakland. The scenery is ugly, industrial. Signs in an enormous font offer divorce or mattresses. Lines of freight cars hold large containers. Semi-trucks and other big rigs rumble along next to cars, vans, and a FEDEX truck. The two-year old toddler I'm going to take care of is the first of a new generation, and her presence sends my thoughts backwards to earlier times, while reality puts me on the 880 freeway.

I turn right and cross the drawbridge, my mind in several places at once.

I want to translate experience into words as directly as possible. Memory has blotted out some things and emphasized others. The past is never totally over, it jumps on my shoulder unexpectedly, mingles with the present, and someone I recognize.

I am repeating a role with my grandchildren. I can feel my mother there behind me, silent. In her last year, she saw pictures of Melissa, perhaps momentarily holding the connections in her confused mind, but then something slipped, and she didn't. Will I be like that?

In a family portrait taken when I was two or three, my sister and I wore our hair in braids, a barrette on one side. My brothers, with fresh faces and combed hair, wore white pants held up with patterned suspenders, and wide-collared shirts open at the neck. I am not smiling, though the photographer and Mother wanted me to.

Father wore a dark suit and a serious face. Mother, in a blouse with a white collar and dark bow, her dark brown hair curled neatly around the edges of her face, smiles with satisfaction. Her family is spiffed up and looking fine.

I've looked at that picture through the years, thinking of change, which vies in my mind with later memories. A late one from 1995 when Mother sat in a wheelchair at the Seattle Airport, her arm gyrating wildly.

"What was that?" I asked, turning to her, eyes large and alarmed.

"Oh, probably a ministroke. I've had them before."

I looked around and wondered if I should call for medical help, but she seemed normal now that the spasm was over.

Later, when I visited Idaho, she sat next to me in the car, looking at me blankly.

"Who are you?" she asked.

******

Now, in my 80's, I look back at my mother when she was young, strong, taking care of four small children, a home, and a small farm, and at the end, confused, unable even to take care of herself. The Kingdom message that she was drawn to when I was a child was her belief throughout life and she had enormous influence on future generations of the family. When, as an adult, I told her I no longer believed that message, she just smiled at me, content, I imagine, to leave me in God's care. After all, hadn't He saved me from the large tire as a child

Chapter Two

Money, Obedience, Parents

I was five. When my sister and brothers returned home from school, we'd run along the ditch bank, shouting at one another, chasing the goats, or watching as Mother slew chickens in the backyard, wringing the neck, then severing the head with one swift swipe of the ax, after which the bodies danced a final, headless farewell.

Once, during World War II, we took a trip in our Model T Ford to Hanford, Washington to see Father, who was working in the defense plant there. Mother brought another woman along to share the rationed gas stamps. Somewhere in the Blue Mountains, we picked up a service man. Everyone did this as part of the war effort.

I had whooping cough at the time.

"Pump her arms," Mother told Ernestine when I had a coughing spell. She would grab my arms and pull them up over my head, then push them down, repeating the action until I quit coughing.

The old Ford chugged away, getting us to Hanford, and home.

During those years, my parents saved enough money to buy property when Father returned. We moved to twenty acres of farmland, with a gray stucco house on one corner of the property. It contained three bedrooms, a kitchen, dining room, and living room, without central heating or a toilet.

On the back porch sat a wringer washing machine and two large tubs. When our clothes had finished the washing cycle, we put each piece through the wringer into a rinsing tub, sloshed them around in the rinse, put them through another ringer, and repeated the process, finally dumping them into a large basket. My sister and I took them outside and hung them on the line. All of this was more challenging in winter, when it was cold and wet outside, and the only option was to hang things inside.

In summer, we enjoyed the screened-in front porch, occasionally sleeping or sitting there in the long, warm summer evenings, with protection from the mosquitoes that swarmed outside. Inside the air was hot and stifling, but on the porch, it was lighter, easier to breathe. I never wanted to go inside. Next to the house were two tall, heavy cottonwood trees and behind those, two black walnut trees.

I've always been trying to meld the inside and outside. It's about openness, about feeling free. Summers were my favorite times. Restrictions, so much a part of my life then, didn't seem as tight outside. No school, and our bedtime slipped a bit, I could read into the night. Remember those warm summer evenings playing tag? Or is it that my ancestors, somewhere deep inside me, lived outside and it feels like the natural place to be?

Beyond the house, there sat a chicken shed, granary, barn, pump house, and a fruit cellar just a few steps from the back door. Mother bought fruit by the bushel in summer. We girls peeled and cored peaches, apricots, plums, and more, then put them in jars. Mother used a pressure cooker to cook them. It seemed like my arms itched with peach fuzz for days after! By the end of summer, the cellar shelves stood lined with quart Ball Mason or Kerr Jars filled with fruit, tomatoes, and green beans.

On the floor would be a one-hundred-pound sack of potatoes, bags of onions, squash or other winter vegetables that would carry us through the season when both work and money were scarce.

In 1946, another baby was born, a brother, Larry. I walked around his crib singing to him. He was like a doll that I would play with but then tossed aside when other interests caught my attention. When I left home, after finishing high school, he held onto me and said, "Don't leave!"

I said, "I'll be back."

He said, "You'll never be back." He was right.

******

Our world was this small, plain Idaho town. Our place, in addition to the farm where we lived, was Hudson Street, where our grandparents, aunt, uncle, and three cousins, who were about our age, lived. We visited often. Ordinary as the wood frame houses along it, the houses on Hudson each had a small front yard of grass, a maple or cottonwood tree, maybe a lilac, rose, or peony bush.

Usually, we went to Grandfather's for Sunday dinner. After church, we would pile in the Model A Ford. With Father driving, we crossed the railroad tracks, turned on to Hudson and into Grandfather's driveway. Then all four doors flew open at once and we jumped out. Running through the front door, I hopped on Grandfather's lap, kissed him and laughed at the tickle from his long beard. Then we kids settled down. We were expected to behave, especially here.

Each Sunday, I helped set fourteen places at the long table in the living room. When it was time to eat, we sat down and waited quietly for the blessing, sometimes stealing glances and giggles if the prayer went on too long. Then, we passed the food politely and ate it without spilling. Improper behavior brought severe reprimand, humiliation, and, later, teasing from the other kids.

The adults did the talking.

"Better get that second cutting of hay in tomorrow before it rains," Grandfather said.

"We'll be canning cherries before long," Grandma commented. Heads nodded.

I was acutely aware that, being a child, I was unfinished. Adults did not get scolded. Adults knew about life, how things worked, and why. We didn't. We stood, wide-eyed, asking for answers to everything, and they were stingy with their knowledge.

Different secrets were told in different places. The women talked while they worked, preparing potatoes, shredding cabbage, and slicing tomatoes. Sometimes, because the girls helped in the kitchen with the more mundane jobs, we caught fragments, leftovers, of something delicious.

Grandma would open the big oven, lift out a roasting pan, turn, and with the steam from the roast beef surging around her face, through the mist, she would drop a couple of words, which like the tip end of the roast, were slathered in rich moisture and innuendo. Pieces of someone's failings—a period missed, a door left unlocked, flesh exposed.

"...wonder what she'll do now?"

"Does her mother know?"

While the women worked in the kitchen—where they usually were—the men sat in the living room, with their knowledge. Their words came out as though through a long and arduous process, methodical, slow, and unemotional. The sound of their voices as patterned as the embroidered white doilies on the arms of the large, overstuffed chairs where they sat.

"How's Truman going to pay for all these things—like social security?"

"Taxes, what else?"

"And, how's he going to keep us from sliding back into a depression, once the soldiers come home?"

"Dunno. Do you have all Jersey cows?"

"Yes...well, mostly."

"Jerseys give the best milk."

Their conversation plodded along with less juice and vitality. No secrets told here! You had to be excited, on the edge of your chair, with one eye to the door. You had to be in a hurry.

The whole being of the men loomed large, strange, and incomprehensible. I wondered sometimes what kind of information passed between them when they talked to the women in their bedrooms—these separate, different people.

We didn't know what else they might do when they were alone. Sex was the biggest secret: the thing we didn't know about and were not told, knowledge more secret than any other, sacred even.

My girlfriend's mother told us we could get pregnant from kissing. The collective message was don't. Don't touch anything. Don't let anyone touch you.

"One day, you'll start to bleed. It will start running down your leg. It could happen anywhere," Mother said, when the experience was inevitable, with or without warning.

After we finished dinner and the dishes were done, we went out to play while the adults visited, snoozed, argued, whatever they did.

Wandering through the front and back yard at Grandfather's, or the short distance between their house and our cousin's place, we had nothing particular on our minds. There was no television. Going to the movies was against our religion, so we didn't have much of an idea what life was like in other places. We played hide-n-seek and made-up games and stories.

"I caught you! Now, you're it!"

"No, you didn't!"

"Let's play some other game. I'm tired of this!"

"This time, I get to choose!"

We didn't know what we didn't know. Sex—what was that?

For years, we were working on a puzzle that made little sense. Gradually, from reluctant adults, from books, from each other, we began to put the pieces together.

These treasures escaped, sometimes from adult lips, sometimes from other kids, rolling through our imaginations like marbles, the agates the boys carried in their overall pockets, pulling the brightly colored globes out at recess to shoot and win.

Once, when we pretended to be old people, I walked bent over and cut my forehead open on the running board of our car. My sister took me inside.

"What happened? What's going on?" One of the adults asked this, unwilling to be pulled away from their quiet repose. My mother cleaned and patched me up. The scar remains.

We played outside at Grandfather's Hudson Street home until late on Sunday afternoon. As evening approached, Mother would come out on the front steps and call us.

Her voice blends now with the echoes of a hymn: "Come home, come ho-o-ome. Ye who are weary, come ho-o-ome."

"It's time to clean up for supper." She would pause. "Then it'll be time for church."

Our innocence gradually gave way as what we knew and did not comprehend changed in kaleidoscopic fashion, like the marbles my brothers played with, rich in color that flashed by with each new turn.

*****

We caught a yellow bus each morning and again in the afternoon. Sometimes, when we returned, Mother had baked bread, perhaps cinnamon rolls. We attacked these with glee, and, because we loved the bread crust, we would, if she didn't stop us, keep cutting until there was only a middle clump left.

Mother learned to bake bread from her mother while they lived in Canada. Later, they moved to Oregon where her mother died. Mother was fourteen at the time. While she was in high school, Mother had a serious ear problem requiring surgery, and she missed much of the school year.

Her father, I've been told, was flummoxed as to how to raise two teenage girls on his own. The family moved to Idaho. Summers found the young women harvesting fruit and living in a tent. Grandfather eventually remarried Dora, a woman who had many children of her own.

Eight years later, as a young woman of twenty-four, Mother married my father, twenty-four years her senior, in a double wedding with her sister at the Nazarene Church.

"Why?" we asked later. "Why would she marry someone so much older and…not a nice person?

"He was very flattering back then," my aunt said. "He bought her all kinds of presents. She got a roomful of presents from him when they were married."

******

"I am the head of the house! You will obey me!" Father yelled at my brothers. "Do what I tell you! Get out there and mend that fence! I'll have your hide!" He turned to my mother, "You, too. You see they do it!"

He was off then, slamming the car door and roaring away. He drove with reckless abandon, so short that he saw the road through the steering wheel. At first glance, it appeared the car was flying along without a driver.

"You better see what you can do," Mother said to the boys, a weary look crossing her face.

Father was the second in a family of fourteen children. After he contracted polio at five, his parents hovered over him protectively. Since he was sickly, he was unable to do the physical labor his brothers did outside in the sun, clearing sagebrush, pitching hay, shoveling manure, or pushing a plow. Nor was he a part of the tasks his mother and sisters did— cooking, sewing, canning, and cleaning. In a time when parents had large families at least in part for their usefulness, most work being of a physical nature, Father was not up to the tasks the other males did. His parents sent him away to college for a time, trying to provide him with a means of making a living. When I knew him—he was 55 when I was born—one leg was turned outward, and he dragged it as he walked.

None of my aunts and uncles exhibited the same temper or cruelty that I saw in him. As a child, I gave no thought to why.

"Do as I say!" My father thundered while we skittered nervously trying to get away from his attention. Not only my father, but all adults, especially teachers, ministers, anyone with authority demanded and usually got obedience.

******

We charged groceries in the winter, then worked feverishly in the summer at fieldwork, an occupation scorned by most white people, as it was usually done by workers from Mexico. But we needed money to live and prepare for yet another winter.

Mother paid the grocery debt with her wages. While not telling us exactly how to spend ours, she asked us to buy clothes, and the school supplies we would need.

When we were kids, I'd hear my dad ask Mother: "What did you do with all that money?"

"Bought groceries, gas, and a few things the children need to start school," Mother answered, her voice diminishing.

"You spent too much. You're always spending on those kids. They should earn their own money. I need more money!"

"I was as careful as possible. We do have to eat."

"I do all the work around here. Nobody appreciates me. You just spend."

She said nothing.

"Answer me!" He yelled at her. He raised his arm in anger, though I don't know that he ever struck her. He was taught that you shouldn't hit a woman, and though he wanted to, he settled for hurling words in an ever-fiercer fashion. From his parents, he also took the practice of the father disciplining the boys, while the mother handled the girls. This saved me in numerous ways—if I wanted to go somewhere or do something, I talked to Mother about it, rather than having to ask Father. By the time I was in high school, Father wasn't well, so he wasn't able to exert disciplinary measures over any of us.

Money was always tight. Once, I went to a candy-making store near the school with some friends. We watched as they made long pieces of what would become hard candy, swirling with red and green. Unable to resist, I borrowed a nickel from my friend to buy a piece.

"You did what?" Mother said, when I told her. "How did you plan to pay her back? I don't have a nickel!" Eventually, she gave me a nickel to pay the debt. I never did that again.

Father took from the church, from his past, and from the Bible those beliefs that suited his purpose: Spare the rod and spoil the child; children should be seen and not heard.

******

When Father returned home near the end of the war, he took a job appraising land for Canyon County, where we lived. Later, he sold real estate. Like his father, he had get-rich-quick dreams.

While selling real estate, Father met a couple whom he thought could bring him the financial success that had thus far eluded him. When they came to our house, Mr. and Mrs. Flinch came with an impressive calling card—a large, blue fin-winged Cadillac. No one along our country road drove anything like it.

As if to match the size of the car, their bodies were large and weighty. They would pull themselves out of the whale-like metallic machine and lumber to the door.

They were friendly in the way people are when they want something. You know that as long as you say what they want to hear, they'll keep talkin' and smilin'.

They persuaded Father to invest in silver. A mine was located somewhere in central Idaho. As soon as they had enough money to get the mine operational, the money would reverse direction and start flowing back to the investors, multiplied many times over.

Father didn't have much money, though he gave them every bit he could, while Mother tugged at the same resources for the care of the family.

Father spent a lot of time with the Flinches, planning, scheming, and hoping. They talked to potential investors, took trips to the mine, and talked some more. They needed more money.

When they came to our house, it was to talk to Mother.

"We know you'd like..." one of them would say, "An indoor toilet. Central heating."

"Wouldn't it be nice if you could...buy meat in the winter or new boots for the kiddies."

"Things will be so much easier for you, when...you have a better stove in the kitchen, another bed for the children."

Mother was having none of it. With a nose that smelled trouble, she knew they wanted the property—twenty acres where the family home was located. They tried to persuade her to allow usage of the property as collateral to borrow money to get the mine working. Both of my parents' names were on the property deed, so they both would have had to sign any such agreement.

She walked around those two as gingerly as she would have a skunk, not wanting the stench to touch her. Polite and kind, she served coffee. However, the pursing of her lips and the way her fingers squeezed her nostrils together meant her answer was, "no." It would always be no.

Chapter Three

Chosen

At the Nazarene Church, I repented repeatedly. Seems like I walked that aisle a thousand times. The categories of sin were vast and attractive, and included bad thoughts. My mind was a seedbed of misdeeds. I didn't actually commit any capital crimes, so to speak, having neither the know-how nor the guts, but I felt as guilty as if I had.

If God planned to take me, I hoped it would be on a Sunday night, right after one of these conversions. It was when I was most likely to be saved. Otherwise, I didn't, as they say, have a prayer.

My experience resembled the one Patsy Cline sang about: "I go to church on a Sunday. The vows that I make, I break them on Monday. The rest of the week, I do as I please. Come Sunday morning, I'm back on my knees."

Heaven and Hell existed somewhere beyond sight, sound, or any map. Perhaps, neither was my immediate destination. God could take me at any time but did not seem in a hurry to do so.

Mother was moving away—and taking us with her—from the Nazarene Church to another church, still Christian of course, but with quite different beliefs. She was making choices that would have a huge impact on us and on generations after us.

We started hearing about God's Kingdom being on earth. We talked about this at home, interspersed with all the other elements of everyday life.

The radio linked us to a world beyond our dirt road, feed-sack-dress, rural one, to people and events barely imaginable. We gathered around it, listening while the Cleveland Indians, Detroit Tigers, or Brooklyn Dodgers played baseball. Those were our favorite teams. We hated the Yankees.

One day, my oldest brother asked Mother, "In God's Kingdom, do they play baseball?"

"Well, I don't know, maybe so," Mother didn't give a fig about baseball, but was interested in God's Kingdom, and the bright possibilities it contained. "If not, there is something just as good!"

Mother studied the Bible whenever possible, talked to other people about it, and heard various interpretations. She needed a promise, a hope of something better than today. Maybe she didn't like the idea of my burning in hell forever. She was searching, beyond the beliefs of the Nazarene Church. Father apparently agreed with her—perhaps because it didn't involve money or disciplining of the children. We were aware of her pursuit. God's Kingdom was going to be on earth! Isn't that what it says in the Lord's Prayer? "On earth as it is in heaven."

When I was about twelve, we left the Nazarene Church and started attending the new one, which wasn't any denomination. We referred to the new beliefs as "the Kingdom Message." We heard about God's Kingdom in every sermon.

My sister challenged Mother. "There is nothing as good as baseball. If it's just as good, if all the good things are in the Kingdom, why not baseball?"

"Yeah," another brother chimed in, "I wanna be able to play baseball."

"Well, I'm sure you'll be happy," Mother said, trying to placate us. Baseball and heaven were distant dramas, stories heard often of unseen things, so both existed by repetition and reputation. The names Roy Campanella, Gil Hodges, Jackie Robinson, and Stan Musial mingled in my imagination with Job, Joshua, Matthew, Peter, and John.

When we played ball in the neighborhood, Mother insisted we play softball, pitch underhanded, and be mindful not to hurt the younger kids. To have enough players meant rounding up every kid in the neighborhood.

"Choose up sides!"

Two boys who were good players chose. They knew who could hit, pitch, catch, or run, and chose those kids early. Once picked, you walked over to stand by your captain. I often stood in the unchosen line as it dwindled, fearing the chagrin of being the last one there, the one the captains argued over which side had to take her.

"Easy out!" the kids hollered when the one chosen last came to bat, or "Hit to right field! She'll never get it!"

Sure enough, in that remote corner of the world, someone would knock the ball to me. I ended up hunting for it in the tall weeds.

Ours was not a regulation field. Sometimes we played in the street, or in someone's yard, or in the corrugated field where running wasn't easy. We used dried cow pies for bases—at least partially dried.

"You shoulda' had that!"

"Next time, we'll make her the umpire!"

I endured the teasing. If I couldn't be a good player, at least I wouldn't be a "cry baby."

******

Learning the Kingdom Message, I listened to new words, phrases, and concepts: the lost ten tribes of Israel...the United States and Great Britain...the British-Israel Movement...a kingdom on earth of absolute justice...the restitution of all things...a Jewish conspiracy..."if my people, who are called by my name will humble themselves and pray, I will deliver them." (This last a quote from the Bible).

I don't remember asking Mother many questions about why we had changed churches. Glad to have escaped the strain of a tortuous future, only avoidable by a kind of perfection that seemed impossible, I didn't question it. We'd also learned to believe adults in authority—a teacher, preacher, parent, policeman, and pretty much any adult in charge of anything.

Over time, I would question all I had taken in, in those childhood years.

Attending a denomination with definite beliefs and then entering a sort of free-for-all in the nondenominational world, I might have challenged what I heard more. However, I went there when I was aged twelve and continued until I was about twenty. Like most young people, I had other things on my mind rather than heavy theological questions. Boys? Sex? Theological questions didn't interest me, so much.

In this nondenominational world, people studied the Bible on their own and drew various conclusions. These people didn't agree with each other about everything that the Bible said. Eventually, I learned most of them still believed in Hell.

What the ones we went to church with did agree on was that the United States and Great Britain were the lost ten tribes of Israel, meant to be servant nations to lead the rest of the world to the Christian God.

Admonished to follow the health laws written in the Old Testament, we didn't eat pork, or any fish that didn't have fins or scales, though with our ever-impoverished state, we'd never eaten crab, shrimp, or lobster, anyway.

We were taught that the Synagogue of Satan is the Jewish conspiracy to take over the world. The Jews already controlled many power centers, we heard, such as newspapers, medicine, money, and much of the government. White Anglo-Saxon people, especially those who listened and believed, were chosen by God. We were the good guys!

It would take me years to realize that the kingdom message I was taught was antisemitic and racist, and blamed the Jews for everything that was wrong in the world.

Mother got books that explained the dire consequences of the people turning from God and of the conspiracy to lead them astray. Everything would get worse and, by the year 2000, life would be quite hopeless. We, the white people who had come here from Europe, were destined to take this land, an idea that led to a U.S. government policy often called Manifest Destiny.

Manifest Destiny, widely accepted in the middle and latter part of the 19th century, asserted a belief that white people were destined to move westward and take over the entire North American continent. This was the justification for moving Native Americans off their land. As far as I remember, I never heard a justification for slavery, but the practice was minimized since we were following God's plan.

However, the moneylenders and other bad actors had gained control. Our only hope was to turn to God for deliverance. He would save us in the Battle of Armageddon. This would happen by the year 2000. Among the chosen was my family—to hear this message and be stewards of it—thereby perhaps avoiding the pain and perhaps even death that others would suffer. That date of 2000—distant when Mother led us into the new belief system in the 1950s—was somehow forgotten as the year 2000 came and went.

After that, we did not get immunizations. Matter of fact, I don't believe we got any shots before that. To this day, I don't think my siblings have received any inoculations. We heard that the shots gave the disease and didn't understand that giving a small dose of the disease immunized one against getting it.

Charging interest, or usury, was wrong, though usary has generally become a term referring to excessive charges. Who decided when the interest charge became too much?

Every word in the newspapers or the radio was suspect—diabolically prepared for the "goyim's" consumption.

Thereafter, as we went about daily routines, we knew something that not very many people knew. The challenge was not to evade a hellish afterlife, but the enemy who controls the government, the financial, educational, and medical institutions in this one.

******

January 22, 2000. It's another gray morning and I'm on the freeway, crossing the Bay Bridge, parking at the San Francisco Airport, riding to the terminal, buying a latte, and boarding a flight for Boise.

Aunt Bertie, Mother's sister—we had grown up with her children—died last Monday. I'm "going back" to Idaho for her funeral, my mind drifting through memories—family gatherings, her potato salad, her forgiveness, and the dry clothes she gave me that day, when I was a kid, when I fell repeatedly into the mud underneath the swing. All these things and more come back to me.

At the graveside service, I wrap my ears in a scarf to ward off the cold. My sister and I greet cousins, brothers, a niece, other family members and friends. The casket, with flowers on top, is suspended over a hole in the ground; green carpeting and chairs are arranged next to it.

A recording of "Amazing Grace" begins the service, played by a fiddler.

"This is not the end," my sister tells the audience. "Bertie will be resurrected when Jesus returns. I think that it may be quite soon. Burying the body is a Christian act of faith that it will be brought to life again."

The next day there is a memorial service. Pictures of Bertie in various stages of her life are displayed. We sing her favorite hymn, "What a Friend We Have in Jesus."

"The Kingdom Message is what she believed," my sister says. "She is the last of that generation. Now we are the older people. We must carry the torch."

My brother, Harry, comes to the pulpit then, to dismiss the service with prayer. Before he does, he reminds us, too, of what Bertie believed, and how fortunate we are to be born into this family, with the knowledge of the Kingdom—of God's people, the Anglo-Saxons, the lost ten tribes of Israel. How some of us are squandering our heritage—both the natural and the spiritual one.

"Each generation is barely surviving," he says. He reminds us how bad things are—a government so corrupt that he does not recognize it, a "de facto government. We will have to have a patriarchy," he says. He has cut the seat belts out of his car to defy the government's demand he use them.

******

When I was about twelve, I went one night with Father to a meeting where J.A. Lovell, a preacher from Fort Worth, Texas, spoke. He taught the Christian Israel Kingdom Covenant message and its fulfillment in the Western European people of today, pastored a church, and published the Kingdom Digest.

His voice was both strong and soft, with a Southern accent. He said things I wanted to hear. "God loves you. Stop worrying about Hell and damnation."

I sat stunned, waiting for the threat, the qualifiers, but none came. For years, I had lived in terror of going to sleep and waking in a burning inferno, the dread growing along with limbs, bone, and muscle, while I was at school, at home, or in church, where it rose like an inflammation.

That night the preacher placed a large doubt in my mind. I cried as he spoke, feeling such relief on the way home that I had no anger even for my father. I slept very well that night.

Chapter Four

Into the Teen Years

If church was an important element of our life, it wasn't all. We went to public school, made friends, and became interested in other things, like music for me.

In fifth grade, two of my best friends played the clarinet. I thought I had to have one, too. I must have said "clarinet" so many times that Mother wanted to get me one just to shut me up.

Still, it didn't happen overnight. Before too long, however, she arranged to buy a clarinet for $120 and pay for it with payments of $10 a month. Black wood, ebony I learned—with silver keys, and pieces that fit together with cork. It was stored in a beautiful red-lined carrying case.

Music was important to Mother. In spite of having to charge groceries at the neighborhood market all winter, she managed to pay for piano lessons. Our responsibility was to practice. For one dollar, Mrs. Stokes taught four of us one-half hour each. A tall upright piano stood in a corner of the front room. On top were pictures of relatives. Sometimes, we stood around the piano and sang church hymns, such as *Onward Christian Soldiers.* Music allowed us to transcend time and space and all the misery this world repeatedly produced.

Mr. Wingling taught clarinet. Eight lessons came with purchase of the instrument. I was to take the instructions on successive Saturdays. I was so excited. I liked Saturdays and could hardly wait to start the lessons.

I took the beautiful new instrument to the music store for the first lesson, and was directed to the basement, where, in a small, closed, set-apart room, Mr. Wingling taught.

At twelve, I was shy, intimidated by all adults and obedient to their commands, so I followed his instructions, opening the clarinet case, with its gorgeous red velvet interior, while Mr. Wingling stood watching.

A thin, skeletal man with long soft fingers—unlike the work-roughened farmer's hands I was used to seeing—he bent near, his body brushed against me as his smooth hands touched the instrument case.

"Lovely," he said, "just lovely."

I felt uncomfortable in some vague way.

He showed me how to finger the clarinet, to fit the reed in carefully, and blow through it to produce music. He gave me a simple assignment for next week.

I returned the next Saturday, still shy but prepared, rarely speaking except to answer questions.

"You have to learn how to breathe deeply, from the diaphragm," Mr. Wingling announced and illustrated by putting his hands against the lower part of his rib cage. I tried, but I was so dumb that he had to show me. And when he did, he lifted my blouse and put his smooth, bony hand on my diaphragm. Then his fingers slowly extended upwards to my breasts.

I turned cold as stone in winter. Goosebumps covered my skin. My just-developing nipples grew rigid. I heard words but could not answer. His very white hands were long, bony, and clean. Those fingers touched me and I felt a strange stirring.

Inside, my known world collapsed. I wanted to leave, to be anywhere but in this little room with this man touching me. Outside, I could be with my sister, looking in store windows, or having an ice cream cone, taking back my innocence.

The sound of another student approaching caused him to move away. Shaking, I began to take the clarinet apart, breaking the thin reed in doing so, feeling his eyes on me.

"I'll see you next week," he said. I caught an emotion, a kind of triumph, cross his face.

The stairs were long and difficult to climb when I left, and the sunshine gave less warmth than I needed.

What should I do? Who could I tell? My sister? Mother must not know. She might take the clarinet away, angrily demand her money back or she might go into the music store and tell the owner what had happened. I couldn't risk either one.

Nampa was a small town, where everyone knew everything about everyone else, and you knew they knew, and they knew you knew they knew, and society was held together by these tenuous, often erroneous threads.

I was afraid that Mother and other people would look at me questioningly. Was I telling a lie? What did I do to provoke him? Mother might become more protective and uncertain about me. Those hands had made me aware of my budding breasts, and some idea that beyond being a child, a world existed, containing mysteries and feelings too complex—and too simple—for me to understand.

Throughout the week, I thought of little else but the coming Saturday. To go again without saying anything might be seen as consent for him to touch me again.

I went. He did. I agonized. There was no one I could tell. No one without consequences.

"I have to leave a little early. My sister is waiting for me," I said when I went again.

"Would you like to invite her down here?" he asked.

"No," I said, looking at him with wild fear.

He laughed.

I tried to avoid being near him, coming late, leaving early, suffering in silence through his groping, until the eight lessons were over. I never told anyone until I wrote it on this page.

"Would you like to take some more lessons?" Mother asked me at the conclusion of the series.

"No, not for a while," I said, looking past her.

******

We had the strangest neighbors. They didn't go to church! I didn't know anyone else who didn't. Heathens. Across the dirt road from our house, portly Mrs. Gentry came outside in summer and stood on the shady side of her house. "Y'all seen the mailman t'da?" She asked this of anyone within earshot.

"He's over near the McCorquedales'," Mother responded, "'magine he'll be here in half an hour, unless he gets to talkin' too much." She was looking for one of us, so had come out on the front porch. Out back, my sister and I were hanging clothes on the line, squinting towards the east where the mailman drove in his stop-n-go, box-to-box pattern. Bending down to pick up another wet garment and a wooden pin, I wondered if a pen-pal letter would arrive for me that day.

Without looking, I could picture Mrs. Gentry seating herself comfortably while awaiting the postman's arrival. We knew each other's habits. Mrs. Gentry never moved her large body unnecessarily. Not particularly tall, her width seemed to start at her shoulders and move downward, increasing in volume to somewhere below her hips, where, ever so gradually, it decreased in the direction of her feet. Those appendages carried the burden and never appeared to pick her up, so much as to push her along. She wore faded cotton dresses, without style or shape, all year round, adding a sweater in winter or one of her husband's old long-sleeved work shirts. Her husband, whose body size was like hers, wore overalls—never new ones—and left one side unfastened, so he could scratch his belly.

The Gentrys' brought their large and random family from Arkansas to settle in Idaho. This hillbilly mélange, like an old and weathered automobile, seemed to be always careening almost out-of-control, yet never quite shattering into a multitude of useless pieces.

We shared other things with our neighbors besides the postman and the dirt road. The rural telephone line connected eight families. Each of the eight families heard their own ring and three others. Any of eight parties might be talking when one of us picked up the phone.

"The line's busy. Hang up!" A voice said as soon as they heard a click. If you were careful about picking up the receiver you might not be noticed at all.

Some people, hearing that the line was in use, were slow about putting the receiver back down, hanging on to the words. Adults claimed they were "just trying to figure out if they were about to hang up."

You could hear all kinds of things on the party line.

"Ya' know that woman on your side of the line—two shorts and a long—I saw her husband coming out of the Hong Kong Cafe with some other woman."

"Are you sure she was with him?"

"Sure looked like it. He didn't get home until late that night. I heard his car when I got up to let the cat out."

"Well, his wife's not been lookin' too good lately. She better tend to her business, if ya' know what I mean, or someone else will!"

"They've got an alligator over there! I just know'd I saw it! Couldn't believe my eyes!"

"What if it gets away? Better not get my chickens!"

"Or worse!"

The party line hummed.

When I went over to the Gentrys' house, a part of me wanted to be there, another part didn't. I hoped to see something that I could tell about later. Mrs. Gentry was often on the phone with one of her children.

"So that's the reason the line's busy," I thought.

Mrs. Gentry sat at the large, chrome-rimmed table in the kitchen, her back leaning against the wall, listening to the telephone in her hand. Sometimes she said nothing for a while, moving the receiver away from her mouth, giving directions to someone in the kitchen.

"Well, 'al be," she said finally, "if that don't beat all!" When she hung up, it was to tell those around her what she had heard.

The kitchen was the center of activity in the Gentry household. Mrs. Gentry spent most of her waking hours there, cooking, or talking on the phone, or questioning her husband about the price of strawberries or eggs. The two children still at home—Lonnie and Lurleen—took orders from her. The dog sat nearby, always on the lookout for any extra scrap that might come his way.

"That hog meat with white gravy and biscuits is gonna kill''em! There can't be anything healthy in it," my mother would comment later when she heard about the scraps.

"Well, I saw the dog running around, kinda strange, yelpin'," one of us would say to add to the speculation.

My family was convinced that such food would kill the Gentrys, or, at least, make them crazy, and we often saw evidence that this was happening. If one of us saw the dog running around in circles, yelping, well, what would you expect from an animal fed hog grease and white flour?

Lurleen was my age, and a friend, off and on. We fought as much as played. I always felt a stranger in that house, though Mr. and Mrs. Gentry treated me politely, and Lonnie ignored me completely in the presence of his parents.

Other people in the neighborhood made comments about this family from Arkansas., which increased my interest in going into their house: "Don't go to church...don't speak right... Lonnie wanted to date a girl, her father said no, Lonnie choked him...hog meat and white gravy...they 'do it' with their own family...with animals...did you see what happened?"

We repeated such comments, retold them until the stories flew on the wind and gathered as proof of our neighbor's strangeness, providing bizarre security against our own oddities.

"Snakes—they've got snakes over there! I saw 'em," my brother said one day as he entered the back door. "They keep 'em in a hole in the ground with chicken wire over it."

"They got 'em from Florida. Mrs. Brown heard Mrs. Exley telling her daughter on the phone. She overheard Mrs. Gentry..."

"They grow 28 feet long and get as big around as your fist!"

Since the Gentrys didn't go to church, we referred to them as heathens among ourselves. Since most people did attend one of the many churches in town, Sunday morning was the quietest time for the party line. Mrs. Gentry did not miss the opportunity.

"She was on the line when I left! She was still on it when I got back from church! Can you believe it? What do they talk about all that time?"

Every year, when we finished school at the end of May, we picked strawberries for Mr. Gentry. Getting up at five o'clock in the morning, we crossed the road, crawled down the wet rows, filling baskets with the red berries.

A nickel for each basket was our pay, and we did fairly well, making several dollars by ten o'clock, if we worked hard. We had to pick the rows clean, not just go for the big berries, and we had to work until the patch was finished.

One day, I was assigned a row next to Lonnie. Five years older than me, he was big and bullied all the kids in the neighborhood when adults weren't there to stop him. As he picked that morning, his hand moved quickly across the plants to between my legs, reaching for my crotch. I jumped and tried to pick very fast and stay ahead of him. Some younger boys watched and laughed as I scrambled. If I didn't pick the row clean, Lonnie's Dad would fire me.

When the last berry was picked, Mr. Gentry paid us. I raced home, delighted with the cash, glad to be away from those boys. Not telling anyone. Not telling, because the party line picked up everything. The echoes bounced through house and field.

Mrs. Gentry would have clucked her tongue in that way she had: "That girl's goin' to amount to no good," she would have said.

******

We lived in a farming community, so we not only picked strawberries, but weeded various crops for local farmers, and detasseled corn.

In late July or early August, the thermometer reached around 100 degrees each day and did not drop quickly. Evenings were warm, until gradually the air that had hung hot and relentless began to stir and cool. The mountains turned monolithic against the escaping light. Over our heads, while we lay in the grass, or hid under a small bush or behind the trunk of a tree, stars appeared, each a small brightness against the night.

One evening, the farmer we worked for, Mr. Allen, called the house and talked with Mother.

"The tassels are coming out. It's time. Can you come?"

"Yes, we'll be out about seven."

We rose early the next morning, pulled on Levis, long-sleeved shirts, and work shoes. Packing a lunch and cold drinks, Mother and we four older kids piled into the car for the drive to the field.

The morning dew still hung on the plants when we began, walking the v-shaped spaces (made for watering) between the rows, our feet plodding along the slanted side, our bodies covered, except for our faces, protection from the sharp edges of the leaves which, like paper, appeared harmless, but could inflict sharp cuts.

Creating hybrid corn meant removing the tassels containing pollen from one kind, so the pollen from the other variety would fertilize all the corn. We reached up to pull the tassels off the tall corn. At the same time, we continually pushed the arching leaves of the corn plants out of our faces. At ten o'clock, we stopped for water, and rested our arms and legs.

"How far will we be by lunch?" One of us would ask. Mother looked at her watch. We figured it out.

"So, we'll stop for lunch at 12:30. That way we'll be near the car," my sister said, "and we will have more than half the day behind us."

We rested in the shade of the front lawn at the Allens' house, by their invitation. The Allens treated us—particularly Mother—very well. They hired us for whatever row crop work they had. We talked, ate thick sandwiches and sometimes store-bought cookies. We thought them better than homemade ones.

"You gonna go to the carnival?"

"I wanna get a car."

"Those carnivals can sure take your money in a hurry. Remember you need to buy school clothes and supplies with what you earn," Mother said. She knew we had to spend part of what we made frivolously but continued to remind us not to blow it all.

"Yeah, but I wanna go to the carnival. Are they gonna have the roller coaster?"

"Yeah, but it costs more than the other rides."

We soon returned to the cornfield and the afternoon's work, walking until we knew every bump and curve, the taste and touch of the plants and dirt. The fine, powdery pollen penetrated our skin, leaving us itchy and raw where it chafed. The sun bore down. Our clothes became sticky with sweat, dirt, and the peach-fuzz-like covering on the leaves.

Sometimes Mr. Allen came out to check and see if we were deflowering the plants correctly. He leaned on his shovel and talked to Mother.

"If it stays this hot, we may have to work the field on Sunday," he remarked, knowing we usually didn't work on Sunday.

"Yes, I know," Mother responded. "I'll check with you Saturday night."

The work was tedious and hot. Still, it appealed to me as a refuge from home and the storminess there, from school, and church. I was uncomfortable in those places. Here, we were a unit, with everyone doing their share and each of us receiving equal pay—75 cents an hour.

As the day grew hotter, we counted the money we would make and talked about how to spend it.

"Boy, I'd sure like an ice cream cone—black walnut and vanilla."

Mother bought groceries and paid bills with her wages. She turned our hours in, got a check from Mr. Allen, and then gave each of us our portion. She argued with Father. He said all the money should be turned over to him and even approached Mr. Allen once, asking for the check, but Mother had anticipated that move, and he didn't get it.

"If they don't get paid, they won't work," she told him.

"Oh yes they will!" He thundered, pounding the table. He and his siblings had given money they made to their parents and continued to send money home even after they had moved away.

As the hot afternoon continued, our spending dreams would grow quieter; the muscles along our arms and legs ached with repeated motion. When we finished, we stood on a high spot and observed the patterned field—the tall bull rows with a white, fluffy, feathery crown above the green stalks, the female rows of pure green.

"Can we stop for ice cream?" someone asked on the way home. The small corner market had milk nickels, creamsicles, popsicles, all for five cents. We chose which one to buy, piled back in the car, munching in silence, or arguing about who would be the first to take a bath.

Chapter Five

Life and Death in the Family

The storm that was my father invaded our lives upon his return from Hanford, and continued, only slowing when his body failed him. I see him now, raging "against the dying of the light," as Dylan Thomas put it. As long as he could, he moved with force. His voice, harsh, sharp and quick, spouted orders at Mother or his children. I don't remember one kind word from him.

For a time after the war, he worked at the county assessor's office. After that, he sold—or at least, tried to sell—real estate. He also tended to the cows, leaving most of the milking to my brothers.

Once, my brother, Harry, helped a neighbor with some work; the neighbor gave him a quarter. He was so proud! He came home and showed it to Dad.

Dad slapped the quarter out of his hand and said, "It takes more than that to feed you for a day!"

Harry looked crestfallen. As he became older and stronger than my father, he stood up to him, contradicting him or refusing to do what was wanted.

"They'll do it or else! They won't live here any longer! See how they like that! I'll throw them out!" He raged about Harry's conduct to Mother.

"No, you won't," Mother responded calmly, almost under her breath. Still, just as you can't miss the fragrance of lilacs, her words prevailed.

She was the balancing wheel that made our lives possible. Always reasonable, she stood between Father and us, negotiating, refusing to let either side fall away entirely.

"Well," she said when our exasperation grew, "well, he just doesn't know how or what to do. He was affectionate when you were babies. He didn't know what to do when you got a little older and had your own ideas. He's good with figures."

We huddled together against him, taking warmth from each other.

"Leave him," we told Mother when we were teenagers. "We'll take care of you."

"Well, now..." she said, but she never considered such a thing.

We connived together against him, making fun of him, deceiving him, and laughing at the futile motions of his life.

When my older brothers, Harry and Stanley, wanted to go to the local rodeo, the Snake River Stampede, they told our parents they wanted to sleep outside in the yard, down near the barn. They made the bedding look as if figures were there.

At some point in the evening, Father decided to go check on them. Ernestine, or Ernie as we called her, fell in beside him and started asking him questions. She diverted his attention.

"Yeah, they look fine," she said, as it grew dark. In the dim light, the cloth figures looked real. The two of them turned around and headed back to the house.

In time, Father's never-strong body weakened. Confined to a wheelchair, he suffered pain most of the time. Codeine had been prescribed, but on a schedule, and the pain always came back before the clock allowed more medication, so he would cry.

In high school, I would bring friends home, walk past my father who was moaning, and say, "Oh, don't bother about him, come on in." Today, I do not like to admit to such callousness.

In and out of the hospital and various nursing homes, Father's health continued to decline. Since my parents had little faith in the medical world, it being controlled by those who were trying to destroy the chosen, they were left to what advice they could gather from other sources. When his illness became acute, they turned to a local doctor and warily took his advice. Father had cancer, but even after surgery, he didn't thrive.

Mother took care of all of us and worked outside the home at night. During the harvest season, she stood picking debris from the food that came by on a conveyor belt at Birdseye Food Products for twelve hours at a time, and when she returned home, took up other responsibilities, so she got little sleep.

We were growing up, moving toward our own lives. As a senior in high school, I worked thirty hours a week at Cliff's Drug Store, just across the street from Mercy Hospital. Each evening, except Friday, from six until ten and seven hours on Saturday and Sunday, I served sodas, milkshakes, and hamburgers at a small counter and waited on customers throughout the store. The owner allowed Mother to buy Father's medication at a discount.

There was never enough money. Mother had no teeth through most of my childhood. They had been pulled when rotten. She learned to gum even meat by cutting it into very small pieces. When my oldest brother went to work, the first thing he did was buy teeth for our mother. And then, an inside toilet for all of us.

As always, Mother did what she had to do, holding the family together by the strength of her will, rallying to each new chore, and never speaking of any of it outside our house.

She wanted us to obey the rules. When we broke one, especially a specific agreement with her, she was hurt. Disappointing her was painful. On those occasions she withdrew, holding something back that seemed essential for breathing. She would go about her work, avoiding eye contact, and saying nothing to the offending party.

Once, I asked to go to a snow party with a church group, Youth for Christ, which I belonged to in high school. I'm not sure why, but she said no. I decided to go anyway. Sleds and toboggans and kids all piled into the back of a truck. On one of the first runs down an icy slope, my leg caught and twisted. Though not broken, it swelled and hurt for days. I was not taken to the doctor and not given much sympathy either. You break the rules, you get hurt.

Some things stay with me, through the years, some I want to hold on to and some I cannot let go of.

"Where do you want to live, Mother?" One of us would ask her years later in a mellow moment.

"I could never live in town. I want to be where I can see across the fields...the horizon, as it was in Canada, endless...the Northern Lights, in summer a spectacular show."

I thought the light was inside my mother, following her form as it does a comet, shredding the darkness, pushing it back.

Mother was born in Iowa. Her family moved to Canada when she was an infant. Her sister, Bertha, or Bertie, as we called her, was born there. The family also included a half-brother, Dewey, who was older than the girls.

After several years there, experiencing the deep and heavy winters, they moved to Eugene, Oregon, where my grandmother died. Mother was a teenager at the time. As a result of illness, Mother didn't finish high school.

I wrote of her later:

Lilacs

A lilac bush grew in our front yard, big enough for hide-n-seek. I thought about it Friday morning while cleaning house. Mother's favorite color was lavender. She always liked that bush. She harvested sugar beets in the chilly Idaho November and celebrated the next month by selling Christmas trees at a lot on Second Street next to a warm coffee shop. Now, lilac blossoms float around my face, the concave irrigation ditch rests in my palm, thirsty grass growing along its banks. The flowers came and went quickly each spring. A cold snap and they were just gone. Clusters, cone-shaped tiny blooms with a fragrance, which, in dreams, she still carries into my room.

All of this time, we continued to go to the Kingdom church. While he was able, Father went to this new church where the Kingdom message was taught, but he didn't lead us in that direction. Mother did. She was all in, and her children followed her lead.

The kingdom would be heaven on earth, everything fair and honest, no one would be without what they needed. After the Battle of Armageddon, Christ would rule on earth. This was the paradise we lived for.

******

In the last two years of his life, cancer sent endless and fierce pain throughout Father's body. The codeine blocked it some of the time, but not all. He howled. At the nursing home, he waited at the front door, in a wheelchair, for a member of the family to come and get him. He wanted to come home and stay.

The winter of 1957 was unusually cold in the Boise Valley. The car would not start one morning, so it had to be towed by someone we knew. We didn't have the money for a tow truck. I was to sit in the driver's seat and steer the non-running car. The car-pulling went very slowly. It was so cold. I don't want to ever be that cold again.

In February of that year, while the ground was frozen and the landscape dead, Father died. While some of his siblings lived nearby, where we saw them often, others lived in Los Angeles. They drove the long trip to be with us at his funeral.

The family that drove the thousand miles to be with us had often come before. Aunt Geneva would take a cup and go to the barn, because she liked milk "straight from the cow," and that was where she was going to get it. They also sent gifts for us children, gum or candy at Christmas. Uncle Dewey took us to the Idaho State Fair. He gave us five dollars apiece. A fortune.

Years later, as a young mother, I visited Uncle Slim, my father's brother. He offered me dates, raisins, whatever he had.

"Your dad was never very well," he smiled in apology.

One of my uncles gave Mother a cemetery plot, so Father was buried in Kuna next to his parents and other family members. A small temporary sign marked the spot for almost forty years.

My father was embalmed. Later, the family decided against that. Believing strongly in the resurrection, as they did, they took to burying the dead just as they were when they died.

Chapter Six

The Road Trip

In May that same year, I graduated high school, with no consideration of going to college—going to work was the alternative. From our religious point of view, college would have taught us about evolution and other things we didn't believe in. Besides, it was a waste of time because the end was coming soon (for this reason, a minister in Texas advised my brother and sister to buy everything they could and charge it)—so to work it was. No matter how lofty a future we saw, money was needed in the here and now.

Before that, however, my older sister, Ernestine, and I embarked on a trip across the country in a tan 1947 Studebaker. On a bare-bones budget, we would visit "kingdom" people. "Kingdom" had become our word for those who believed, as we did, that the Anglo-Saxon people were the lost ten tribes of Israel and that when Christ returns to earth, he would establish his kingdom in the United States and Great Britain—over time it would fill the entire world.

My sister had done the planning—had written to kingdom people, set an itinerary, and saved most of the money. Our purposes diverged: She went for the "fellowship of kindred minds" and to preach and learn more of the gospel. I went for the adventure, though I was not averse to the company we were to keep. I was a believer, too.

We would stay with these like-minded folks as much as possible. We couldn't afford many nights in a motel. Our brother cut a piece of wood to fit the space between the front and back seat, padded it and added legs, so one of us could sleep while the other drove.

In 1957 the freeway system had not been built. We headed east on U.S. Route 30, staying with a couple in Laramie, Wyoming, who had birds, so that while we ate, the birds dived in and around us, swooping over our heads.

We laughed about that for days afterward. Whatever else might have been caused by our family setting, laughing was what we did to relieve the pressure of being strange, poor and poorly dressed, with few redeeming social graces. Often, our humor was at someone else's expense.

"Put a man's hat up behind the back seat, so people will think a man is with you," our sister-in-law's mother had advised us. At four o'clock in the morning, the police stopped us as we wandered, lost, in downtown Philadelphia. They wanted to know where the man was. Skeptical of our explanation, they implied that we had done in this fictitious man, but they still let us go.

We were put up for the night and treated hospitably in many homes across the country. "Green" and "lush" come to mind when I think of the twin cities of Minnesota, where we visited some believers.

On a Sunday morning in June, we drove through village after New England village, listening to church bells and gazing at narrow steeples and people walking toward little white churches. Picturesque and pretty as could be.

We went to Massachusetts to meet Dr. Howard Rand, the editor of Destiny Magazine, about as big a guru from our world view as possible. We were greeted warmly—a wonderful raspberry sauce lingers in my mind. Someone in the congregation took us in for the night. The great man, too, was gracious and welcoming. I was glad for such encounters. Being part of a small, select group who knew the truth had great appeal to my family: until that time, we had little about which to distinguish ourselves.

Stopping in New York, we heard the Reverend Billy Graham preach at Madison Square Garden. Though we didn't agree with everything he preached, we admired him. We felt some kinship with other protestants. Catholics, not so much. And, beyond that, well beyond the Christian world that we knew, lay darkness, heathens, and nonbelievers. No hope out there.

In Washington D.C., we visited the Senate and watched Senator John F. Kennedy and Idaho's Senator Henry Dworshak. Someone steered us to a wonderful and cheap place to eat—where house members dined. Our minds overflowed with the sights.

We passed through the Smoky Mountains and the deep South. Our car did not have much get-up-and-go in the mountains. Once a man in a military uniform followed us for hours because the car kept stalling and he knew how to get it going. At the border of Louisiana, we were served the darkest, thickest, and strongest coffee ever. Delicious.

In Dallas, Texas, we went to Dr. J.A. Lovell's church. He was the minister who had come to Idaho and told us to stop worrying about Hell, so I always had a soft spot for him. At home, we received his Christian family magazine, *Kingdom Digest*, monthly.

While in Texas, we bought a delicious watermelon for a half-cent a pound and ate as much of it as we could, as fast as we could, having no way to store it.

At each of the places we visited, the people were warm and welcoming to us.

Somewhere along the line, I heard a former Communist talk. Communism—the bear that, we believed, would come against God's country. The evil of it. A former Communist told tales of rape, breasts being cutting off, death, devastation.

Sometimes I could not sleep.

Chapter Seven

A Young Woman

It is August 2006, a morning in Benicia, California, with clouds holding back the sun's hard edges. From my condominium, I overlook the boats and yachts in the marina, the Benicia Bridge, and the Carquinez Straits, where enormous ocean-going vessels glide through the water effortlessly.

Ducks, sometimes snowy egrets, live here; migratory birds stop enroute to another place. Along the water's edge is a walk and bike path. It is a constantly changing, yet peaceful, scene. In the evening, with the light dropping, pink sometimes hovers near Mt. Diablo to the east. Often the water is quiet, the scene tranquil. Blue sails and American flags waver.

In this setting—so different from my early days in Idaho— I return to my transition from being a child to becoming a woman. At home, most decisions and rules were made for me; each day on my own, I began to move into my own choices, sampling this, testing that, finding out what worked, and gaining strength in my instincts, even questioning some of the things I'd heard in church.

The trip with my sister was a hiatus. The next thing in my plan was being on my own, living away from home. That meant having a job, being able to pay my own way.

In this quest, and to visit my friend, Jackie, I went to Mud Lake, which, though still in Idaho, is 250 miles from the Boise Valley. I even got a position as a waitress at Woolworth's in nearby Idaho Falls. I was fired in a couple of days, as I didn't know the lingo—"mayo," "BLT," "over easy"—and couldn't keep up with the pace demanded. I returned home to Nampa.

Boise was the nearest "big city," at least by comparison. Then and now, the older sections of Boise retain a measure of grace and elegance, though new office buildings have swept away some of the two-story houses and the trees that lined the streets in front of those dwellings.

The wide boulevards—Warm Springs Avenue and Harrison Boulevard—are lined with trees, and behind them, well-kept lawns and shrubbery provide a green and opulent setting for the large old mansions. Some are a Southern style with round columns across the front, while others are New England clapboards with paned windows. These were the addresses of choice in those days, with their atmosphere of romance and permanence. Inside those carefully draped windows, I imagined bright, happy, beautiful people lived who knew what to do and did it properly.

My sister had worked for the telephone company in Boise, which helped me when I applied for a job there. I was hired to work in the mail room, probably the lowest rung on the totem pole. I lived, for a while, with my sister in an apartment over a garage in Boise, renting from some people in our local congregation.

When my sister went to Canada, I moved into a ground floor apartment with Jackie. This marked the beginning of change in my life: exposure to many other young people, to making my own choices, to questioning all that I had learned. To have fun!

Soon we lived in an apartment on Washington Street, a block behind the Idaho State Capitol. The location made it easy for me to walk to work—at Mountain States Telephone & Telegraph Company. I would cut through the capitol grounds, often nodding and saying hello to then Governor Smylie, who returned the gesture.

The ground floor apartment ran the length of the wood-frame building. Near the front door, a metal receptacle held the mail for everyone in the building.

Noise might have been an issue, except we never let on that the landlord brought other women in while his wife was at work, as he knew we could. We made friends with Poppy, the elderly woman who lived above us. She rapped on the floor at midnight when music and laughter from our apartment awakened her.

We rapped back on the ceiling.

The next morning, she would come out on the landing and say, "That racket! How vill I sleep?" She asked this and shook her Polish fist at us. She was short and stocky and had pure white hair.

"We're sorry, Poppy! Next time, you come down and join us!"

"'Vat you mean? An old lady like me!"

"Sure. The guys will love you."

They did. The smooth and tan college boys who visited while on vacation from school leaned over her small frame, flirting outrageously.

"Hi Poppy! How ya' doin'?" Our friends hailed Poppy whenever she was seen in the hall or on the walk in front of the house. She learned the names of several of our regular visitors.

The dental student studying in Kansas named Barry was her favorite.

Jackie was a favorite with the men who came to our door. Barry used all his charm to win her attention. Others were attracted to her, lost their heads, and seemed to see nothing in their vision but her thick, dark hair; her high, sharp cheekbones; her beautiful tawny skin; and her large brown eyes. She came from Oklahoma, and rumor had it that she was 25 percent Native American.

I made friends with people I admired. Jackie fit that description. When we were in high school, I hung out at her house as much as possible. We played clarinets on her front porch, joined by her uncle and his trombone. The neighbors must have gone crazy. We sang duets at church, each attending the other's church on occasion. When she moved to Twin Falls, I was devastated, but we stayed in touch.

In high school, I was fat, at a time when body image was important for women. My kind and slender roommate, with all the male attention she received, served as inspiration for me to slim down and begin paying more attention to fashion.

Her family had an Oklahoma casualness and warmth that drew me like a cozy hearth, contrasting as it did with my life among sharp edges and biting tongues. She had never learned meanness, but possessed a generosity of spirit, and a hearty laugh. I loved to hear her chuckle.

At the telephone company, I was the mail girl. I had to sort the pieces that arrived and deliver them to the appropriate office. Simple enough, I was shy and felt uncomfortable walking into private offices. I wondered if I should speak to the person—it was always a man—who sat at the desk, or should I remain silent. The latter seemed somehow rude, the former presumptuous. I was relieved when the occupant was on the phone or talking with someone else.

I was quite serious as I walked through the various rooms. In the large rooms filled with many employees, I did not look at or speak to anyone unless they spoke first. Later, when time and experience had made me more relaxed, a co-worker said she had thought I was "stuck up."

I laughed: "How could I be stuck up? I'm nobody."

Eventually, I was offered a position in the payroll department. I recorded hours by hand, overtime, and deductions, and calculated paychecks. When we were told that the office would be closing because accounting procedures were moving to Salt Lake, I was offered a job in another department in customer service. I flourished there as well. It seemed the telephone company had more confidence in my abilities than I did.

Jackie and I walked to work, to the grocery store to shop, and to the post office, which soon became an important stop for me. Often, we met for lunch in one of the small downtown cafes. Gossiping, giggling, telling the stories that unfolded at work, or talking about the fellows we were seeing or wanted to, we hurried through the meal and returned to work.

Alcohol had been forbidden in the Nazarene Church and, I guess, it was assumed to be an evil in the second group of believers to whom I belonged. I don't remember hearing anything about it. Now independent, we began experimenting. Some adults were always willing to make a purchase for us at the state liquor store. We took care of each other—if someone drank too much, we made sure they got home safely. Our parties were usually at our house or nearby, so driving was not involved. Once, I drank seven shots of vodka with coke chasers. Jackie and my boyfriend *du jour* walked me up and down in front of the house until I began to sober up.

My life was fun and exciting. Work. Home. Dating. Each place had its intrigue, personalities, and discoveries. I was running my own life, and I liked that. As young women, we had an unspoken agreement. Whatever plans we had made, if a man called and asked one of us out, we dropped the plans we had made with each other. At times, we had other roommates, and with all of them, this cardinal rule applied.

Years later, we would ask ourselves, why? We would marry and have children. We knew and accepted this just as we had accepted the absolute divine origin of the Holy Bible. Putting a priority on male-female relationships seemed natural.

Marriage was a possibility filled with mystery. We were enamored with the idea. The romance. The excitement. We were not totally impractical, however. Jackie worked at a finance company, and for a while, I collected final bills for the phone company, so we talked to the folks at the collection agency frequently. We checked on men we met. If a young man did not pay his bills around town, he would not make the cut with us either.

So much did we believe that marriage was our destiny, we looked upon those few women of our acquaintance who had never married as failures. If we didn't marry, we, too, would be failures in this primary life task.

In high school, I was not only overweight but, according to my brothers, I was dumb. I had few dates in high school and was very fearful that I would end up an old maid.

After I married, years after, I had nightmares about being alone and lonely, thinking the two were the same, fearing this. Sometimes I woke up dreaming that I was alone and had to lie there and reassure myself.

When Mother heard us talking about young men, she was quick to point out, "They only want one thing!" She spoke of all males.

"How much will she put out?" We knew this was a question that the guys asked other guys. The prettier, the more desirable, the more unattainable object could afford to be more standoffish. Awkward, unattractive, shy, or stupid girls would have to put out more with less expectation of return. "Putting out" was contrary to the moral principles with which we had been raised.

At the telephone company, two young married women in the accounting department said they would like to introduce me to their brother.

Ronald was tall, dark, handsome, and slightly pudgy. He lived on the large farm his family operated near Nyssa, Oregon, and ate meals prepared by his mother—designed for full-time hardworking farm hands. He drove over to Boise regularly for several months while we dated. He was a decent sort. The best possibility I had at the time. Men were measured in possibilities: was this someone I could introduce to Mother?

I was compliant and sweet to Ronald's family. One Thanksgiving, at his house, I offered to wash the dishes. They let me. I did everything possible so they would like me. Still, he dumped me. I felt hopeless, really, as if I would never get it right.

On Saturdays in the warm weather, Jackie and I cleaned our apartment and did the weekly grocery shopping, then sunbathed in the backyard, trying to become perfectly brown all over. Taking a clock with us, we turned ourselves regularly, lathered cream across our bodies, and talked.

In May, or as soon as the stark Idaho winter departed and the blooms of spring gave way to the warmth of the approaching hot summer, this tanning process began, and it continued until sometime in September, when the leaves began to fall. Various friends joined in this pursuit. When someone with a car offered, we drove to Lucky Peak Dam or Idaho City or a pleasant spot along the way. Near Morse Creek or the water of the dam, we soaked up the sun like something we had to have. When autumn came, we watched the carefully cultivated color fade away. The next season, we started over.

Our circle of friends included other young women and the men whom we dated, as well as men who just came over to visit. I found I liked bouncing ideas, opinions, and views around.

Much of the conversation was trivial. Elvis's latest hit. What should I wear on Saturday night? Some of it was serious, however. I found myself exchanging opinions and asking questions, beginning an intellectual curiosity beyond what I had known. I moved from being told what the truth was to testing whatever position was asserted.

The beliefs that I grew up with were still very much a part of me, but when I explained them to others and they questioned me, some pearls of doubt dropped through my consciousness.

Are you sure? What about how we took the country from the natives? And enslaved Black people to do the work? Why don't more people know about this? Are some people better than others because God chose them?

So many years later, with a lot more experience in life, I thought, God chose one people? Any parent knows that if you had one child and told the others that the one was "chosen," that is, was your favorite, all the others would hate that one. Did the God of the universe take that into account when he "chose" one people above others. Or was it men who wrote it down, men who didn't have much experience raising children? Men who thought that telling their people they were chosen would make them feel special. If the tribe was special, people would be very devoted to it, would give their life for it.

I attended church—if irregularly. I tried to believe and behave, but was drawn, at the same time, to a world that could be light and frivolous, not so filled with dire predictions.

"Did you park?"

"Yes."

"How long?"

"Oh, it was after the movie. I don't know. Fifteen minutes, maybe."

"Did he try anything?"

"Oh, you know. They always try something." A giggle.

"Have you ever been caught by the cops? They like to patrol lover's lane, you know. Like to sneak up on you. I think it's kind of sick."

"Did he try to put his hand under your blouse?"

"I wore that pink one that tucks in. Why can't they just kiss?"

"Well, you know, they are different. They always want to do more."

We talked like this all the time. What the guys wanted to do was what we were not supposed to do, could not, if we were to continue to be the kind of girls our mothers had raised us to be. Nice virgins.

Our own desires were secondary in this struggle of how to hold on to a male by giving him enough so he would come back, but not too much. If we gave him all that he wanted, he would be gone, or so we feared. This was before the pill. Pregnancy loomed large.

What did we desire? How strong were our sexual impulses? I did not think these urges had any legitimacy at all. Was not the body evil—only the spirit redeemable? Outside marriage, at least, sex was wrong. I was not sure about kissing and petting. I was not going to ask.

In the novels I read as I grew up—Jane Austen and the Brontë sisters—"making love" was coming to call on a lady. In her long, voluminous gowns, she received gentlemen callers with a nod of the head. Conversation was foreplay to a touching of the hand or a dance. (I had been told the evils of dancing.)

I don't know if we had any other role models. My mother—as far as I know, just about all mothers—didn't go into detail about behavior while dating. I think she would have been pleased had I not dated at all, or at least until I was thirty. God's plan for my life was marriage and children, but the untidy specifics were never discussed.

I did not fear Hell anymore, but wished to be "good," to be loved by God. Still, my body responded to warm caresses and kisses. Physical contact of any kind was rare except on a date.

"God gave us these impulses, but we aren't supposed to use them. I don't understand," I complained to Jackie.

"I don't know what to tell you, but the woman is always in control. She has to be. You know he isn't going to stop unless you make him."

Jackie's friend, Barry, brought various fellows over for me to date because Jackie was more likely to go out with him if it was a double date. First, he brought what he described as an "Italian cowboy." (I didn't understand the incongruity in that description).

We all visited in the living room for a while, then I excused myself and went into the bathroom. I didn't want to go out with this guy, who was quite a bit older and didn't appeal to me. When I did not return, Jackie came looking for me.

"What are you doing?" she wanted to know when I let her in.

"I'm not going back out there."

She giggled. "Come on, I. It won't be that bad. We'll be together."

"No."

"Why not?"

"I don't want to go out with him."

"Look, I promise. We won't park. We'll stay together."

Silence.

"What am I going to do with those guys sitting out there?"

Finally, I went. He did not fit the picture in my head. He was not dirty, or rude. He said nothing lewd or inappropriate. While he drove, I talked about the lines in the middle of the road, their color, and length.

Jackie roared with laughter, later retelling the story.

Then, Barry brought over another college fellow. Roy was blonde, very smart and polite. We began dating. His sense of humor was biting and sardonic. He loved the outdoors and took me fly fishing.

I was almost good enough for him. He recognized my mind as well as my body. We saw each other as much as possible on all his school vacations and exchanged letters daily while he was away, first at the Wharton School of Finance and Commerce in Philadelphia, then at Stanford as a law student. With such credentials, I should have known, the end of this relationship wouldn't be a happy one for me.

During this time, I continued to please the telephone company. I was given training and became a customer service representative, a position that had some status among the employees.

The company offered to pay 80 percent of the cost of any college classes employees chose to take. By now, painfully aware of my limited education, I began taking classes at what was then Boise Junior College.

This step did not meet with the approval of the minister of the kingdom church I still attended.

"They will fill your head with ideas. Not with Biblical truth. If you go to college very much, you'll never be back," he said. He was right. He said it softly, this fatherly, wise man, who was kind even when I did not follow his advice. I did not want to disappoint him, but I was interested in all kinds of ideas. I wanted to know what it was "they" were going to put inside my head—as if my brain were a receptacle subject to filling by anyone who happened by.

I enjoyed the classes. I had tolerated twelve earlier years of required schooling like a sentence without reprieve. Now, I leapt into this new discipline with excitement.

A Shakespearean actor who performed each summer in Ashland, Oregon, taught, in his rolling and theatrical style, the words of the Bard of Avon. I was mesmerized.

Jackie's boss owned one of the large homes along Harrison Boulevard and offered to rent the adjacent apartment to us. We found ourselves living on the street I had earlier coveted. Jackie began dating her boss's brother, and within a year, moved to Omaha where the rest of his family lived. I was desolate. When they were married at the Catholic Church—Jackie converted— I refused to attend. Catholicism, so I understood, was about as bad as pagan worship.

At work, I was promoted to Business Office Supervisor.

Roy and I were "pinned" for a while. He encouraged me to take classes and develop my mind. Even if it was not good enough for him, it should not be wasted. While he was at Stanford, I learned he was dating someone else, so our relationship ended.

We had dated for two or three years, so the breakup was painful. I was alone again, but not quite as much without resources.

Work had become a source of pleasure and stimulation. As a part of management, I was treated with respect. The level of management which I attained was Level One. Women were not considered for positions beyond Level One and a Half.

Management, particularly beyond the beginning levels, was totally male. I trained men who were paid more the day they walked in than I was after being employed there for years. I was used to deferring to men, but as I grew and changed, taking on more responsibilities, I began to question what anyone said, male or female. If it seemed wrong, or if I didn't understand, I asked.

The idea that male knowledge and opinions were more valid than female just never seemed right or accurate to me. Maybe I got some of this from my mother. Not exactly the words she said, but what she did. My father had his narcissistic viewpoint: Mother cared about us.

She wasn't a feminist. She would have denied that word throughout her life, but she was honest, fair, and a good judge of people. And she didn't automatically defer to men. She stood up for what she thought was right, especially when it involved her children.

But maybe she was not such a good judge of religious ideas that were presented to her. This came to me so much later.

For all my religious training, I never had really been taught that men were smarter, or better, or should be in charge. I suppose it was in the culture, but having a weak father and a strong mother didn't make me believe I should defer to men. I'd worked for men, of course, and I could take orders, but I never experienced men as being demonstrably smarter. Mostly what I heard was, "It's right because I said so!" Does that ever convince anyone?

Chapter Eight

Reimagining the Myth

What if a woman had written this story? How might it be different? Oh, I'm sorry. I forgot. Women weren't allowed to read or write. They were made for domestic life.

Her guilt is the original myth. Would all people throughout the centuries, had it not been for her, have lived and walked in a perfect place? Or would there have been no more people? Would the two of them, had it not been for her susceptibility, have lived innocent forever, or for a long time? How long was forever, in the original text? Was it everlasting, or simply longer than we can imagine or count?

In another time, he might have been a military leader: he understood about following orders without question, especially from the top. He understood the importance of discipline, of rank. He roamed about the garden with a full stomach, without touching the apples. He never questioned the apple thing.

When he slept peacefully, curved into himself, in the shade of, say, an oak tree, he sometimes ran his fingers over the place where his missing rib had been. This is where she had come from. She was no doubt, lesser than he, having been made from one bony rib. Smaller, newer, different somehow. Did he ever think that she would be his downfall?

Did her creator, who made her with all she was and was not, choose that she be subject to temptation? Did he give her free will to make her own choices? To suffer the consequences? Why has her sentence gone on so long? What is the statute of limitations on eating a forbidden apple? She will be subject always, forever— how long is forever? —to God's law and man's law. She will not be the maker of law: she will be the subject of it.

Physically smaller and typically weaker, she will be his property, his whore, his wife, his lover, his servant, his slave, his right hand. He will have dominion over her and she will feel it. If her master is cruel and unjust, she will suffer physical abuse, verbal derision, lacking any opportunity to justify herself, living in the cesspools of the world. If her master is kind and generous, she may live very well. She may sit on satin cushions and have others wait on her. He may even give her freedom. Still, where can she go and have it as good as she has it here? On the soft pillows? All she must do to keep up this cushy life is to be compliant. Is that so much to ask?

What of her crime? Was it victimless, or did we all fall in this seemingly harmless act? The harm was in breaking the law. We respect the law, understand the importance of it, of obedience. Still, where would we be had not someone, various ones throughout the ages, chosen to question a command. Living on a flat earth that the sun circles. One person is the legal slave of another. One class of people with more rights than another, the divine right of kings. Did she do it in the name of everyone who would feel the need to test the limits?

Did she just want to experience a new taste?

On a particularly hot, but perfect, afternoon in the garden, Eve was restless. She had wandered through the entire area, past olive and yew trees, past hibiscus with huge red flowers, had caressed the fragrant roses with no fear of thorns, had smelled the lilacs, the jasmine, had climbed the branches of a cottonwood as high as she could reach, looking for what lay beyond the garden, beyond what she knew. It seemed that the lush, fruitful, and blooming garden continued endlessly.

She climbed down with a sigh, blind to the beauty around her. She had never experienced anything else. A desire grew in her: to live, to experience, to know the unknown. To discover something else. Something she couldn't identify brewed just beneath her surface, never used in this paradise: she wanted to feel! To hurt and heal. To laugh or cry. To be surprised or amused or amazed.

There was an order, a system. She was put there and told to obey. Something, somewhere—was it the serpent, or what the serpent represented? —some small stirring within said question. Push the limits.

With an intuition beyond her experience, she thought of the apple tree, the fruit of the knowledge of good and evil, and she wanted it. She craved life beyond what she had known. Never having known evil, she had no fear of it, or any reason to value what is good. She had never felt the hot, murderous heat of the Gobi or Sahara Desert, so was unaware of the protection afforded her in this place. She had never been hungry, or thirsty, or scared, or lonely, thus, to be filled, to drink, to be secure, to have companionship meant nothing.

She went toward the apple tree, remembering the command. Why were they to stay away from this tree of knowledge, of good and evil? In that moment, she was experiencing what she knew not, what few ever know: a beneficent world of beauty and plenty, of comfort, of safety.

As she went toward the serpent, toward temptation, she walked for the first time with purpose, with anticipation, eager to learn what this great mystery, this unknown, this forbidden thing was.

Adam was lounging on the ground, listless, a little bored, when she came by.

"Where are you going? Why are you moving so quickly?"

"I'm going over to the apple tree."

"Why?"

"I want to taste it."

"You can't do that!"

"I know of the command. But, why not?"

"I don't know. Why push it? We have everything we need."

"What is need? I'm so restless. There's nothing to do, no reason to get up in the morning."

"Yes. I know, but we have been ordered not to touch that fruit. We have everything. What is your problem?"

She continued walking and he followed behind her, wringing his hands, trying to dissuade her, though he could give no reason other than the command. He knew nothing of penalties or consequences. He didn't even know they were having their first argument.

"Stop. Don't go there. Don't do this. What do you want, woman?"

She stopped for a moment, turned to him: "You can't tell me why not. I don't know either. You must understand. I feel no peace in this place. A restless spirit has overtaken me. I will claw the bark of these trees, bury myself beneath this dirt, or jump from the highest branch soon if I can't get out of here!

"Something tells me that all the pulse of life is in that tree and maybe the opposite of life, as well. Going toward it, thinking about it has awakened so much curiosity in me. Can't you see—for the first time I am going someplace, not merely moving about, I am looking forward, whatever that is."

She took his hand. "Feel that beating within me! Something inside has awakened! My life is about to begin!"

Chapter Nine

A Marriage

"This one is different," Maxine, my roommate, remarked when I returned from my first date with Tom, "I've never seen you like this before."

Tom and I worked in downtown Boise, so we passed each other frequently during the lunch hour. Quick looks were exchanged, a slight show of interest. At a nightclub, Joe's LB, we saw each other—each of us with another person. Tom knew the man I was with, so the next time the two men saw each other, Tom asked for my name.

The phone rang one evening—in yet another apartment, this one in a quiet circle where trees stood above the buildings so the sun never shone clear through. I was preparing a dinner of Kraft Macaroni and Cheese. It was Tom. We talked for a while. I agreed to meet him for coffee.

On that first date, I learned he had grown up in nearby Caldwell, graduated from the University of Idaho, and was president of Sigma Nu Fraternity in 1958. It would be a long time before I knew another story about his fraternity, but I'll tell it here, because it says a lot about the man he was.

Tom, as a freshman being inducted into the group, had a wooden paddle used on his butt until it broke. All new initiates received this treatment. That paddle—broken and tied together with masking tape—hung in our garage throughout his life. As a senior and president of the fraternity, he ended the practice.

When Tom finished college, he joined the military. The draft was active and he decided to get that obligation out of the way. For eight weeks, he was in Fort Benning, Georgia, for training. When the group he was with was finishing up, they decided to have a party. They went to every restaurant or bar in the area, but none of them would allow the party in because there was a Black man in the group. They didn't have a celebration.

Never philosophical, but a man of action. Still over the years I found that, in addition to his quick sense of humor, he was ethical. He didn't talk about it. He just was.

Also, he was fun to be around. I must admit, I was hooked from the first date.

Even the credit bureau in town, whose owners were now familiar to me, sanctioned this man. "We met him years ago. He was this cute little guy who pulled his red wagon around the neighborhood. You couldn't do better!"

He was tall and slender with a mellifluous voice and polite manners. Always clean and neat, he reflected the Danish Swedish roots of his parents. He took me to meet them one evening, casually, remarking that he had to pick up some papers at their house. Did I want to ride along?

When we arrived, I met his mother, a small blonde woman who taught third grade in Caldwell. His father was bowling that evening. Tom disappeared downstairs. His mother and I visited. She was taking classes at the College of Idaho (eventually renamed Albertson College), a few blocks away, to get the equivalent of a degree. Earlier, she had attended normal school to get a teacher's certificate.

Eventually, Tom's father came home. Dark-haired, wiry, and energetic, he worked for the Idaho Power Company and belonged to the Lion's Club.

I think maybe we all had coffee and cake. At any rate I was comfortable. They were warm and friendly.

Another day, while we danced together at Joe's LB, he sang "That's All," in my ear. "I can only give you love that lasts forever." He said he was in love with me. There, on the dance floor, I responded with, "We'll see." Some faint and distant voice tried to gain my attention. I ignored it. I was gone.

That was in the fall of 1963. We were engaged in two months and married in another two—running away to do so. Tom didn't care about having a wedding and I was aware of costs and the involvement of family members pushing and pulling at me to do it in various ways.

We married in a simple ceremony in Twin Falls, Idaho, before the Methodist minister and two ladies brought in as witnesses. The next day, we drove to Reno and tried to find a room. Because it was a holiday weekend, we were not meeting with success when we saw Tom's parents walking along the street.

"We're married!" We announced, pulling over and greeting his parents.

If they were disappointed in the elopement, they did not show it. Instead, they gave us their hotel room.

The only part of me that seemed not in a mood to celebrate was my mouth. My gums swelled. I could barely eat. The dentist, back in Boise, said it was stress related. He prescribed medication, and advised me to stay on a bland, liquid diet.

I barely minded. With the diet, I lost ten pounds. I could never be thin enough.

The family, God and the church, and the government agreed. Formerly repressed sexual desires were now approved. I always thought it funny that such a basic urge was so frowned upon—was a sin, actually—until marriage.

Many years later, I visited temples in India with carvings depicting every possible sexual position. It occurred to me how different that view was from the Christian faith that completely separates spirituality from sensuality. Is there any possible intersection?

A young woman told me later that when she met Tom at a party and he had asked her to dance, she declined, deciding, "He will never settle down." As it was, Tom—who appeared too dashing and too good-looking to be married—was ready to have a home and a family.

Tom's employer viewed his marriage as a sign of stability and gave him a raise. I, on the other hand, was seen as a short timer. The law of averages insisted that I would be pregnant within a year. I did not disappoint.

Tom, his parents, and my mother were all at the hospital that Monday evening in early March when our son, Anthony, was born. I saw wild joy in Tom's eyes. Evenings, returning from work, he would stop by his Aunt Blanche's house a few blocks away to say, "Most beautiful baby ever!"

We began building a home in one of the new sections of Boise. Tom's father drove over every night after work from Caldwell, to work with Tom until late in the evening. They spent months painting the house. The painting constituted the down payment for the house.

When Tony was a few months old, we moved into the new house, bringing what furniture we had managed to buy. Our dreams were limitless.

As my family spent much of their energy studying the Bible, thinking of another world, Tom's family was involved in this life, in reality.

Rather than deploring the commercialization and non-Christian aspects of Christmas, they enjoyed the season. Never putting an emphasis on expensive gifts, they cooked fine Danish cookies—shortbread and a thumbprint variety—and tried to see who could wrap a gift in the most innovative way. They drank specially mixed daiquiris, cooked together in the kitchen, feasted, and laughed. Aunts and uncles, dressed in their best, came, carrying candied sweet potatoes or a tin of cookies and small packages for everyone.

"One time," his parents said, "when we were first married and didn't have much money, we decided we would make fruitcakes and give them to our friends and family. We bought all the ingredients—butter, nuts, whiskey, and raisins—spent all day cutting and mixing, before putting the dough into small pans. We put them in the oven but failed to adjust the time so it would be right for the small containers. We ruined the whole thing! Burned to a crisp! The raisins were like little buttons! We were so disappointed. Finally, we shrugged our shoulders and went out to a movie. What could we do?"

On Christmas, a centerpiece of red candles surrounded by greenery decorated the table. The dishes were the Rosenthal China that Tom had bought while stationed in Darmstadt, Germany, by the US Army. His mother had asked him to buy her a tea set while he was in Europe. He did. Then he continued to buy more.

"The women who worked at the china shop got to know me," he said. I could see them smile as the young American came in to purchase something else, perhaps the covered casserole dish, until he had a complete service for twelve.

"You should take them," his mother said to me when we got married.

"No, he bought them for you," I said. The dishes eventually came to our house when his parents died. Now he is gone, too. The dishes remain.

The holiday was jolly and bright. I was taken in, accepted and welcomed. I liked all this and didn't really want to be a part of the conversations my family would so frequently have—about the dire state of the world, the evil systems, the future Armageddon, which they didn't think was that far away. From their viewpoint, nothing that seemed good to me really was. I went with my instincts toward light and joy.

At that time, I wasn't ready to change my beliefs; however, increasingly, I lived my new life without giving as much thought to my family's beliefs. I liked the life I was living. It didn't seem bad. Instinctively, I went toward joy.

Our new, carefully painted house was situated in the middle of a new subdivision in Boise's "bench area." The mountains curved around the northeastern side of downtown Boise and a plateau formed the south and west edges, creating a bowl where the old part of the city was. As the community grew, people began to build on the plateau that circled the south and west area. This development along the bench spread west towards Meridian and in every direction.

It was 1965. In our neighborhood, young men grew lawns, made babies, and worked. The sky was blue and extended endlessly above us. On clear nights, the dark canopy was dotted with stars.

Entertainment was television or, on weekends, endless and silly card games. Tom settled into marriage with enthusiasm—rarely going out with his friends, though he had said he wanted to do that one night a week. At his job and at home, he worked hard. Daily routines of going to work, dinner, and time with the baby, watching television from the couch, making love, and going to sleep to awake to the same routine the next day, were natural and satisfying. Though raised a Methodist, he did not believe in God, in Heaven or Hell. This lack of faith did not trouble him.

"Maybe I'll take a class at night. I was going to night school when we met." I said to Tom one night, early in the marriage.

I was sitting next to him on the couch, where he watched his beloved sports. To be heard, I spoke between plays, or during a time out. Otherwise, he might raise his hand to ask for silence.

"Oh, okay. Are you going to take cooking and sewing?"

"That's not what I had in mind."

"That's what seems useful. What else do you need?"

"It's not so much what I need as what I want," I murmured, but he was back into the next play.

"I have to fire Betty tomorrow. The district manager talked to me about it today," I said later.

"So...?"

"It's hard."

"But you have to do it?"

"Yes."

"So, that's that."

I had not made the decision to fire the employee, rather was directed to do so. The young woman tried hard but failed in the training class. I wanted her to succeed just as I never want to throw a plant out that has one glimmer of life. Also, I didn't like the unpleasant task.

Having no choice, I met privately with Betty.

"I've been praying that God would help me do the job," Betty began.

"Ah, well," I said, clearing my throat, "I don't think it is going to work."

"Oh?"

"I think it is time to stop trying. Find something you are more suited to."

Betty reached over and patted my hand. "It's okay. I'll be all right."

On the weekend, Tom washed the car—the new 1963 Chevrolet Impala he bought just before we met and married. He raked, planted grass, and watered the ground faithfully and watched it nervously for six weeks. Finally, the sprouts were visible. Tiny green blades began to change the brown to green.

Though I had vowed earlier that I would not marry anyone who was not a "Kingdom believer," I had. Though Tom was unabashedly what he was, and smoked and drank as well, both things my mother hated, and though she had never really wanted me to move away from home and get married, she liked him. He teased her, talked to her about the corn crop, never picked a fight, or behaved rudely.

His family, too, liked mine. It was one of those inexplicable things. In over a quarter of a century of shared family picnics, feasts and celebrations, of meetings large and small, casual and formal, as far as I know, there was never a harsh word. No attempt was made to convert Tom's family to the "Kingdom Message." The two families enjoyed each other and had mutual respect. That was enough.

At the time I met Tom's family, babies were being born. Both of my sisters-in-law were pregnant at the same time I was, so the joy and the job of having little ones, raising a family, and taking care of a home took much of our attention.

I loved my life, except that I wanted to talk to Tom about more than the necessities and could not find a way to do so. I needed to explore verbally all that was going on in my mind and the world around. He was uninterested in conversation beyond what was pertinent. He worked hard at home and for his employer and did not care for more than that.

He drove the blue and white Chevrolet to my office each evening. When I saw him coming, I jumped into the car with enthusiasm.

"How was your day?" I asked.

"Oh, fine. Yours?"

"Oh, this customer got really mad and Carolyn didn't show up for work and..." I rolled along telling him the minutiae of the day. He listened but never wanted to share trivialities from his experience.

While he did not consciously deny my need, neither did he share it. There were always "things" to do and television to be watched. I wrote him a note once, trying to express this need. It alarmed him. He came quickly to the bedroom, flicking the light on to see if I was there.

What did the note say and what did we say to each other? Years later, I wrote another note. He turned angrily toward me: "If you have something to say to me, say it!" He threw the paper away without reading it.

Most of the time, other aspects of life overwhelmed what felt like a small, private, and unimportant need. I was loved and cherished! His parents liked me! His aunts and uncles were nice! I had borne a perfect little creature—a part of myself—that lifted tiny arms toward me.

With some pangs of guilt, I rarely attended church with my family, and consequently, saw them less often because so many of their gatherings were for Bible study or worship service.

As I was a voracious reader, someone suggested I read Michener's Book, *The Source*. I read about the elders of the tribes of Israel writing the Books of Moses, the first five books of the Bible, as I knew it. Michener simply wrote about the process, not saying whether the words were inspired by God or not.

Maybe before that, I'd just thought these Biblical books floated down in one piece from God. Now, the physicality of picturing real people—men, of course—putting pen to paper brought the process down to earth in some way. And, coincidentally, God had many of the attributes of men—at times, angry, vengeful, jealous; at other times, loving and caring.

I see this as a pivotal moment in my thinking about what Christians call the Holy Scriptures. As I grew and asked about translations of the Bible and how did we know the King James version was an accurate one, and what about the books that were dropped along the line—the ones with goddesses in them—people said to me, "God made sure his words weren't corrupted."

As much as anything, the patriarchal nature of the scriptures, as I came to know, them planted doubt in my mind as to whether these much-translated words were indeed the words of a supreme being.

Chapter Ten

California, Idaho, and Change

We arrived at the San Francisco Airport in September 1965, at the same time as the Beatles, with considerably less attention. Tom was transferred; I was thrilled. Just the name San Francisco made me think life was more exciting there. It had to be.

"You'll need to wear a hat there," some older ladies had advised me. I bought two, but in the quiet suburb where we rented a duplex, hats were hardly necessary or appropriate, particularly the formal ones I'd bought.

That first California autumn, greenery and pyracantha berries protruded in profusion along the narrow and curving roads that led to the little community of Moraga where we settled. The East Bay foothills stood close and present, in contrast to the mountains I was used to seeing in the distance. Winter did not come on as it had in Idaho. Some leaves turned, but many stayed green and, with the beginning of the rainy season, grew shiny with moisture.

In Idaho, after the brilliant color, there was a lack of color, though often beautiful snowy days in winter. In California, the seasons changed with more subtlety.

Tom left for work early every weekday morning. Knowing no one, I read whenever I had extra time. Truman Capote's "In Cold Blood" put me into a depression for a month. Taking the stroller for Tony, I walked the sidewalks and paths of the little community. Tony crawled out of the stroller, shoved my hands away, and pushed it himself. When he was tired, he climbed back in and I pushed him home.

Tom's cousin, Neil, who also lived in the Bay Area, visited us occasionally on the weekend. We played games and talked about serious things, sometimes. As in debate class, which I had enjoyed in high school, these conversations helped me develop reasoning skills and test my opinions.

In less than a year, Tom was transferred again, this time to San Diego, and before long, we bought a new home in a new suburb on the San Diego/La Mesa border.

Again, as in Boise, landscaping was needed. In the balmy San Diego climate, everything grew year-round. People planted in a desert motif with rocks and gravel to ward off the insistent growth. Washers and dryers were placed in the garage, as it was never too cold to be out there.

The night before our second baby, Philip, was born, Tom's parents arrived with gifts for everyone and lavish praise for everything we were doing: having babies and establishing a home.

While Tom worked, traveling frequently for the company, I changed diapers and cared for Tony and Philip. Soon, even going to the bathroom was not done without a child following me. Sometimes their incessant demands strained my patience.

Their lives changed me in significant ways. I grew up with sin, a very real and tangible presence. The flames of Hell had been painted hot, wide, deep, and almost inescapable. The most I could hope for was time before the inevitable. By the time I was twelve, and someone told me that I didn't need to worry about Hell, I was relieved, but the earlier images still bounced around in my head, stinging, taking the joy out of enjoyment.

Part of the original packet of beliefs I was given was the doctrine of original sin, according to which, we were all born in sin. Born sinners. I believed this. The birth of my children changed that inside me. I simply was unable to believe that they were born sinners.

Coming out of a primordial soup, my boys carried characteristics from me and their father, and our parents, and back, and further back. What does all that amount to? How free were these two babies to be what they chose? Jung talks of the collective unconscious; perhaps that is the source of all instinct, feeling, and judgment. We shake hands because our ancestors did so, illustrating that they had no weapon, and the grasp is with the right hand because the left hand was known as the toilet hand, the one ancient people used to wipe themselves with. Or do we shake hands because we learned the custom? Nature versus nurture, or perhaps the two work together. It isn't a contest at all; humans work with what they have, what they started with and what they accumulate.

These two children had the capacity for evil or good, depending on what I did and what others did and how they reacted, and what they did, but they were born innocent. All the rest comes later. To believe that is to go against not only what my family believed, but what has been a principle of Christianity from the beginning. Christ died for our sins. Millions have chosen, or been cajoled or forced, into believing this. People repent and repent and, oh, yes, repent again. Still do.

The subtle philosophy that our nature is flawed from the beginning is illustrated in many hymns: "I am weak but thou art strong"; "Amazing grace, how sweet the sound, that saved a wretch like me"; "What a friend we have in Jesus, all our sins and griefs to bear." Even if we accept salvation, we are always supposed to be humble, never totally saved from our base natures.

How much responsibility does anyone have for what happened before they were born? Whatever the answer, on a gut level, I no longer believed in original sin. It evaporated in the San Diego air as I held and cuddled and fed the children. I lost patience and yelled at them. Then, I hated myself for doing it. However, I saw nothing malevolent in their natures. Quite the contrary, these small children were innocent.

Tom wanted children to adore and cuddle, but he wanted them always under control. He earned the money. I took care of the children. When he came home, the house should be clean and the children, too, ought to be neat and orderly. It wasn't always that way. Sometimes when I lost my temper and realized it was not their doing, but my own frustrations, I told them: "I'm sorry. It's not you. I just have a lot on my mind."

Still, as Philip crawled around the floor, seeming to leave a spot of curdled milk everywhere, I had the love affair of my life. On the floor with them, building with wooden blocks; bathing them in the evenings; reading a bedtime story while they sat in my lap in their fresh pajamas, leaning their softness against me. I thought that all good, loving, wonderful possibilities existed in these children.

Tom's relationship with them was different from the beginning. He adored them and played with them. "No," was a word he found unnecessary to repeat often. When he said it, he expected and got immediate compliance—something I did not always receive. He thought it was because he was firm. I thought it was because he wasn't there all the time, did not deal with a thousand small incidents every day, and, because it was not my nature to be so absolute with them.

I did not want to be the absolute "it's right because I say so" and "do it because I tell you to" parent. I wanted to be reasonable.

******

Across the street from our house in La Mesa, a San Diego suburb, a woman and her children lived. Her husband was in Vietnam. She had four children, one of whom had some disabilities. Her responsibilities overwhelmed her. She found a sitter and went shopping. Often, deliveries came to her door. I watched the woman carry in numerous packages from the car, giving directions to the errant children as she walked towards the house. When her husband finally returned, they sold almost every piece of furniture in the house to pay the debts. Tom and I bought the dining room table and chairs and the large hutch that matched. Frequently, we heard yelling before the family moved away. Later we learned that the woman had spent time in therapy trying to gain control of her life.

She was the first casualty I knew of that war that soon occupied the airwaves and television in a major way. I went to a prayer service for the crew of the Pueblo, a U.S. Navy ship captured by North Korea. Talk radio became my daily companion as I took care of the house and family. The ideas and sounds followed me from room to room while making beds, vacuuming, and caring for the boys. I ironed everything. I wanted to be a perfect wife.

Opinions, reports, and tempers flew out of the radio and the world moved into my little sphere, insisting that I pay some heed. Women burned their bras and young people like me protested the war in city streets across the country. Whole and new thoughts opened with the possibility that my country might be wrong. Raising boys, I asked myself: what cause would be sufficient for them to be sent to war?

One night a week, I went to night class. Tom didn't mind, seeming to understand my need to get occasionally. Literature was my favorite, eventually history and political science were on that list.

Once, when Tony was about five, I went to the grocery store, and he rode along. We went to parks frequently at this time, so, no surprise, when he saw a large green area, he asked: "Why don't we go to this park?"

"It's not a park. It's a cemetery," I replied.

"What's a cemetery?"

"Well, it's a place people are put when they die."

He didn't ask anymore, but it came to my mind to say something about resurrection. I couldn't say it. In the minutes before we got to the grocery store, I realized I didn't believe that these bodies would be brought back to life in the future. I was crying when we went in. This recognition was a break from what I had heard, from the beliefs of both churches I had gone to.

Why was I crying? I couldn't just believe things because a book said them, even the Bible. By now, I knew that people who believed in the Bible varied vastly in what they believed and how they acted upon those beliefs. Still, it was painful to pull away from my family. However, I would eventually feel about what I had been taught, the initial breaking away was painful. Believing the Bible is the word of God is an act of faith, not of fact. I was losing that faith, and gaining faith in my own instincts, feelings, and experiences.

I didn't just wake up one morning and say, "Well, I don't believe what I grew up being taught." The people who had taught me the second set of beliefs presented it as beneficial for us and for everyone, eventually. They believed all would be well when everyone was aligned with God's word and rules.

Learning about other beliefs is somewhat like learning about different countries. I continued to read, listen, and think. If I had stayed in the small circle of believers I grew up among, maybe I wouldn't have questioned them because they put their faith in certain books, apart from the mainstream. I didn't.

Religious people want to ban certain books. They understand the power of ideas. So do I! That's why I want a world of books and libraries open to all ideas. All dictatorial regimes limit access to news and ideas. The Nazis burned books. The Taliban and the Iranian patriarchal government restrict what can be read or taught. In Florida and other states, books are being banned. I left the faith I grew up with because I had access to different ideas, different experiences. Access to information is vital to understanding the world.

******

Before Tony started kindergarten, Tom was transferred to Riverside. From 1965 to 1974, we moved six times. Each move brought new excitement. The company took care of the cost of selling and moving. Tom got a raise and a promotion. His life was his job and his family.

The family was my life, as well. Still the daily routines of dishes and diapers, and more dishes and diapers, made Tom's life of business travel, lunches, and promotions seem exciting. I had some envy. He put in the sometimes-tedious hours without much comment, but I knew when he was going to take a trip, which seemed much more interesting than what I was doing.

I liked moving, relished the challenge of a new neighborhood, new surroundings, new, new, new. Fresh ideas were popping in front of me; the women's movement waved its banners. I listened.

Each time we moved, we bought a home in one of the up-and-coming suburbs favored by young executives and their families. We wanted our children to be safe and to attend good schools and for property values to be secure and rising. California was exploding with such conditions.

When we bought a house in San Diego, we took advantage of the GI Bill for financing. It would be years before I knew that people of color couldn't do that, and that "redlining" kept them out of various areas. Apparently, that didn't happen where we lived In La Mesa, because we made friends with neighbors, a Black family who had a girl about Tony's age. Her family realized the fine line they walked, living in a mostly white neighborhood. When the other kids were out playing, perhaps barefoot or in older, worn clothes, she came out with her hair fixed in braids and her clothes clean and ironed. Her parents knew she couldn't be allowed to look scruffy. We took turns carpooling the children to preschool. It took me a long time to get the whole story and to realize how privileged we were.

******

I lived in my reality and, though the responsibilities of children and home kept me quite busy, my mind insisted on exploring. All that I had heard in the time when I moved from a frightened-of-hell twelve-year old to a question-everything young woman meant I could not ignore major political and spiritual questions. I could not be apolitical. Probably that's what Tom would have liked me to be, since at times I challenged him. I re-registered as a Democrat. He would always be a Republican.

These were years of domestic—if not bliss—at least good times. Below the unchanging surface, however, revolutionary movements were taking place. I was listening and questioning every absolute idea that I had been taught. The Vietnam War, the civil rights movement, and the women's liberation movement made me think, if not act. I would never be the same again, would never view the world as naively. Written words became the way I explained things—first to myself.

Leaving the Faith of Our Fathers

From time to time, I took a writing class.

Chapter Eleven

Becoming Myself

Each summer, we drove across the deserts of California, Nevada, and Idaho to visit our families in Idaho while the heat shimmered in waves above the asphalt.

"One hundred and six degrees! Can you believe it?" I read as we drove past the thermometer on the bank in Caldwell, Idaho. The downtown area had not expanded much, though homes grew in a widening circle around it.

Old Highway 30 connected Nampa and Caldwell—a wide six-mile stretch of road lined with muffler shops, all-you-can-eat restaurants, used car lots with huge signs and big pick-up trucks parked out front, and whatever other commercial establishments chose to exist in such ambiance.

Karcher Mall—"It's just as pretty as it sounds" someone said—brought people from all around. A wide expanse of concrete for parking surrounded the enclosed stores. The mall's southern side was near Highway 95, the road that took us back to California, through Marsing; Jordan Valley; Burns

Junction; McDermott; and Winnemucca, Nevada, where Interstate 80 connected to Reno and California.

Tom had grown up in a small brick house in Caldwell. He had walked to school. His father could walk to work.

When we visited, Bud, as Tom's father was called, flooded the front lawn. Tony and Philip would play in the irrigation water, while their grandfather worked to corral and control the water's movement.

Tom's parents hosted a picnic in the backyard. Aunts and uncles drove over from Boise. Everyone came to see us. Tom's father barbecued steaks and chicken. Tying a kitchen towel around his middle, he dashed in the back door and up three stairs to the kitchen for something he had forgotten, then zoomed back. With a beer in one hand and a long fork in the other, he presided over the gathering.

"Are you doing the pancake breakfast at the rodeo this year?" Uncle Verne asked him.

"Oh, yes. The Lions always do. It's coming up pretty soon now."

"Second week in August?"

"Yes. I think so. That's about right."

"Will you do the cooking?"

"Help out anyway," he said, turning a piece of meat, adding a little salt. He had been in the CCCs—the Civilian Conservation Corps—in the 1930s and had been the cook for his group.

It seemed like Bud, knew everyone in town, all the habits, rhythms, mannerisms, and problems of the little community. Who was related. Who was out of work or didn't pay their bills. Who was reliable. Who was not. He knew where to get the best deals on most anything and where to buy apples, strawberries, peaches, and pears in season. He would bring potatoes home in a 100-pound sack, and he knew how to fry them up too, with onions, next to a freshly caught and cleaned Rainbow Trout, garnished with a slice of lemon. Two or three slices of fresh, skinned tomatoes. "Can't buy a better meal than that," he would say.

In the backyard in those summers, we talked of everyday life. We admired Tom's Aunt Marg's yard—filled with every kind of blossoms—tall dahlias along the fence that separated her from the next-door neighbors in North Boise. Petunias, clematis. Blanche had allergies, so her yard was green only and Herb kept it perfectly mowed and trimmed.

While our boys were in public schools, some of their cousins in Idaho were going to Christian schools. (Some of the kids that went to the Christian school got involved with drugs while there.) Others eventually went to Oral Roberts University in Tulsa, Oklahoma. Some didn't graduate from high school.

Not many comments were made about the Vietnam War, though protesters rallied, and every day people died there. If it did come up, one of the uncles would refer to those "yellow-bellied cowards who don't have the guts to fight like a man." Whoever said it, the other men agreed. I did not comment, though, wondering if a few years hence someone would want my sons to go to war, knowing I would lie, cheat, or steal to keep them from it. The women rarely said anything about politics.

Visiting my mother's home, I was more strident and argumentative.

"I don't think we should be in Vietnam."

"We shouldn't be there unless we are there to win," one of my brothers countered.

"Right," the other chimed in, "like in Korea. We shouldn't have stopped at the 38th parallel. MacArthur wanted to keep going, but they wouldn't let him."

"Well, we shouldn't have been fighting under the United Nations. The international money lenders control everything."

Tom smoked a cigarette and listened. He was the only person Mother ever allowed to smoke in her house. She saved an ashtray for him.

"I-I don't think it is as simple as all that. Nations need to work together. I don't think you can prove that stuff about the money lenders," I said.

"Well, you have to look in the right places. It won't be in your major news sources."

"And, how do you know your sources can be believed?"

"Because they aren't controlled by the international bankers."

"I don't believe that. I would have to accept your premises and your sources only. I've no place else to go." I looked to Tom for help here. Sometimes he made a remark, but he was not eager to enter the fray.

"I don't have any reason to believe your sources any more than you apparently don't believe other sources." Tom said coolly, exhaling so the smoke curled upward above all of them.

"Manifest destiny," one of them said. "God led us to come to America. Joseph is the vine that goes over the wall."

"So that makes it right to enslave people and take their land?"

"I'm not saying the way we did it was right, but we were supposed to take the land."

"According to who?" I asked.

"The Bible. A scripture about the tribe of Joseph going over the wall. Genesis 49:22."

"Well, that's a leap. One Bible verse and that makes everything we've done okay."

More reluctant to differ with Tom, my siblings might say, "Well, I'll give you something to read," but soon the men were talking baseball, which was their comfort level. Tom, after all, did not grow up with them, had not heard "the truth" preached as we had, so they were willing to be a good deal more patient with his lack of understanding.

Because of their beliefs, my birth family discounted anything I said about Native Americans or slavery; they believed we did what we were destined to do. When I pointed out problems with that, my siblings would say, well, we may not have done everything right, but we were supposed to take over the country. For me, how we did it and who was hurt in the process was important. I couldn't get past that.

When we took the road south, it was perhaps a relief for everyone who stayed and those who returned to California. The trips were both necessary and devastating to me. I talked and cried most of the way home, wanting to be close to my family, wanting to agree with them, but no longer able to. Tom listened as he drove. Seeing how upset I was, he tried to help.

"That's the way they are. That's what they believe. You aren't going to change them. It's better not to talk about it at all," he said finally, when we had exhausted the subject.

By the time we reached Barstow, on Highway 395, those family differences began to recede. I slowly admitted that Tom was right. I could read, investigate, and learn for myself, but could not share my thoughts, questions, and ideas with my siblings in Idaho.

******

The trips to Idaho connected us to our families and to our past, those deeply sunken roots inside us. At home, change fomented inside me. Tom, in a business suit and tie—a similar blue or gray suit and red tie, such as President Bush would wear, with wingtip shoes—went to work early. He set the alarm for five o'clock and came home between six and seven in the evening. One day he would tire of it all. The corporate dream would die. He would give the suits away. The fit was not that good.

The people—and much of the environment, as well—that we saw in Idaho seemed stationary and solid. We saw a bumper sticker one time that said, "Welcome to Idaho. Turn your clocks back 25 years."

I was forming a new belief system, a process that continues throughout my life. I could not stop it or, I should say, I didn't want to stop it. On some level, I accepted what Tom said about my family — that nothing would ever change.

I shared so much with my brothers and sister. We felt the pain of poverty and harsh criticism from our father. We laughed together, but it was frequently the mirth of mutual hurt.

******

"Louie Dumbrowski," my brothers used to call me when we were kids. I hated being called that. In their view, I was fat, dumb, and not very good at softball. I felt inferior to everyone. I don't know if I would ever have moved past that image if I had continued to live in Nampa.

Around this time, my sister, who was a school counselor in Vancouver, British Columbia, quit that job and returned to Idaho, with plans to speak about the Kingdom message full time. She traveled around the country and to England preaching the message.

Sometimes, she encountered opposition. Some thought she shouldn't be in the pulpit because she was a woman. Others objected because she didn't preach about hell. She didn't believe in it, but taught "the restitution of all things," based on Ephesians, Chapter one, Verse ten: "That in the dispensation of the fulness of times he might gather together in one all things in Christ, both which are in Heaven, and which are on earth; even in him." I liked that.

While I didn't share her faith, I thought her views were somewhat benign. She never talked about whites being better than other races. I didn't connect her beliefs with white supremacy, though I knew some people in these groups held more extremist views. As I've said, without a denominational structure for organization, people came to these meetings with many and various ideas, eager to share their opinions.

******

Meanwhile, our lives in California moved forward. I took care of the home and family, as well as taking classes and working toward a degree. Acutely aware of my lack of formal education, I also enjoyed learning, as I had not as a child. My children, too, challenged me to be my best, just by their being.

Tony was ready to start kindergarten in San Diego when Tom was transferred to Riverside. In quick succession, we moved there, then to La Canada in the Los Angeles area, back to Riverside, and, finally to Northern California in 1974. Tom was the ideal corporate man: bright, hard-working, results oriented. His reward was to be moved to the home office in San Francisco, where he became a Vice-President. Tony was in fourth grade, Philip in first.

I took as many classes as possible at Diablo Valley College and then went to San Francisco State University to pursue a degree in English, specifically, creative writing, emphasizing poetry.

I must admit I partially chose poetry because it is usually shorter. I was raising a family, maintaining a household, so I had lots to do. I've never regretted this choice, even though I've written more prose than poetry. Individual words are given more attention with poetry. I think this was excellent training. Two instructors in particular influenced my writing,

Frances Mayes, before she became famous for writing *Under the Tuscan Sun,* was one of my teachers. This delicate, southern woman had fine-tuned instincts and helped me learn about the careful use of words.

Nanos Valoritis, another professor, was from Greece and a member of the Greek royal family there that was able to get out during the coup of 1967. A brilliant man, he had studied in Paris. He lived in Oakland. His home was burglarized several times. He told me they took the television or the stereo, totally ignoring the books, some of which were valuable first editions.

Nanos was a surrealist, and a major mentor to me, opening parts of my mind I didn't know were there. He didn't mind if students fell asleep in class, as he figured they were getting what they needed. Surrealism, and its connection to abstract art, encouraged freedom of thought, an expansion of the imagination.

Since that time, many writing teachers have taught methods similar to automatic writing, as the surrealists called it—free association and stream of conscious are examples—which have helped me. Some things surrealists have published are not for me. I see their approach as part of a practice, a way into what I want to write.

As an illustration of what I mean, I'm going to put a couple of poems in here that I wrote early in my surrealist practice.

The Rapid Transit

After seven, the personality changes,
the night comes in, takes every third seat.
Across from me, Barbie, in red
white and blue, reads a Harlequin novel.

Leaving the Faith of Our Fathers

Over her head, a woman is screaming:
"Is the train always so loud? Where
Are the police when you need them? What
Am I to do?" She searches among the
Chronicles and sleepers for something
to hold on to...

She takes my eyes
and will not let go. I nod,
while Barbie's eyes snap, sharp
and open every twenty seconds.
The woman hands me her despair
in a plastic bag.
I recognize it as my own.

My eyes drop and roll down the track
with the beautiful poems from my lap.
This is the evidence used against me
in court. For the defense, I have children,
someone to meet me at seven-thirty.
What am I to do?

At 19th Street, she takes her diet soda
and leaves. I expect relief,
but my right hip has turned to stone
and her tense jaw is carved there.
I can cover it up.
I can still make love, only slower.

The business suits pick up their neckties,
the Chronicles fold into themselves,
the words moving into place
for tomorrow's edition.

Surrealism allowed me to write down things that I didn't know I knew. As I've talked about in earlier chapters, I didn't see my father as much of a father. Unkind, self-centered, he didn't know anything about raising children. Here is what I wrote about him early on:

Father

When you died
I was washing my hair
I paused
Rinsed it again

Finally
The dead-standing tree
Fallen
Leafless as stone
Hollow as an O
Finished
With the wind's howl
Famished
By the dust
By the sun
Dry as paper

A child
Running toward you
Saw
A trunk
Branches for climbing
Toward others
Hiding places, lookouts

I jumped
Into your emptiness

After studying surrealism, I began to write about my father. I saw him as a young boy. He'd had polio as a child, and it affected his body and his perception of himself. I saw him among his larger, stronger brothers. I felt his inadequacy, measured against his muscular brothers. It was the first time I had compassion for him. I've had a more nuanced view of him since I experienced him in a new way.

Writing has been a voyage of self-discovery. I took debate in high school for a year. We looked at both sides of one topic. Sometimes, we took one side, sometimes, the other, an excellent practice!

******

While I was enjoying opportunities to learn about writing and practicing it, Tom's life was very different. We seemed to meet at intersections, sometimes for glorious conjugal visits, sometimes to glower at each other. I was on the outskirts of his corporate world. I did not really understand it. Though he was a part of family life, he did not live in the daily details of groceries, game schedules, the kids' friends, and house cleaning that I did. My writing was foreign to him, something I dabbled in, perhaps. Could anything that didn't earn money have value? These different life experiences, over time, led to substantially varying opinions and worldviews. In some ways, we led separate lives.

He lived with what he knew, what he could taste, touch, and feel. I wanted to delve into mysteries—the obscure, the spiritual, the unexplainable, and the fantastic. I wanted to talk about ideas. Much of the time, he was too tired to talk about anything. He liked sports and could listen to or watch ballgames for hours, often following different games on different TVs in various rooms of the house. I did not give a flip about football or, eventually, any spectator sports, besides tennis, which I played.

As many of the beliefs I had grown up with dropped away, I turned to poetry to answer the unanswerable questions.

Once, after we weeded for hours in the backyard on a Saturday, I asked Tom if he would go to a poetry reading with me In San Francisco.

Reluctantly, he agreed, throwing off the old clothes, showering, dressing casually, in a sports jacket and slacks. When we arrived at a cafe on Haight Street in San Francisco, he looked around at the small and motley crew gathered there and observed: "Why did I get cleaned up?"

Why did I ask him to come to something he had no interest in? I was trying to shore up the union. Always, I wanted him to understand poetry, my need to question, striving for a deeper knowledge between us, on many levels. I still wanted him to recognize my mind. Praise me, please! He'd been following the corporate path for a long time, and that way wasn't so shiny or hopeful as he reached midlife.

He just wanted us to *be*. He didn't need what I did. It needled him that I kept pushing.

Frequently, when our family sat down for dinner, someone described something that happened to them, or an idea they had heard, and others commented, argued. The children could disagree verbally with us. They had no fear of expressing an opposing viewpoint. These conversations were not "in your face" or insulting confrontations; nevertheless, there was a spirited exchange of quips, ideas, and issues. Tom was a Republican; however, that was around fiscal issues, not social ones. On the latter, we agreed.

Tom sometimes coached the boys' baseball teams, but it was hard for him to get home from work in time, so more often he watched from the sidelines, and encouraged the boys. Though he loved sports, he did not pressure the boys to do well, or even to play. He was never harsh or critical if he had a word of advice. School, friends, and sports were all a part of the children's lives, but what gave them stability and strength, as their bodies grew and changed, was this family unit, a kind of wall. The feeling was not a momentary impression, but one that grew in the children in the same way their bodies developed, a steady, sure increase over time. You might get in trouble within the family, but a sense of belonging persisted.

As I thought about that family unit, I remembered Marianne Moore's poem, "The Paper Nautilus," where she describes the creature that

> ...constructs her thin glass shell.
>
>   ...a dull
>   white outside and
>   smooth-
>   edged inner surface
> glossy as the sea, the watchful
>   maker of it guards it
>   day and night; she
>   scarcely
>
> eats until the eggs are hatched....
>
>   ...the intensively
>   watched eggs coming
>   from
> the shell free it when they are
> freed....

...like the lines in the mane of
    a Parthenon horse,
    round which the arms
    had
wound themselves as if they knew
love
    is the only fortress
    strong enough to trust
    to.

The structure stood while the children grew and remained strong, even with the trouble that came when Tom's and my words and worlds collided, after having knocked against each other for years. I would wonder about it years after he was gone. We got married too soon. Did not know each other well enough. Given that, did we do as well together as we might have? Perhaps I could have done better. The ever-more-frequent nights when he stopped for a drink after work should have been a sign. He didn't know how to express his frustrations. He could have talked more.

When he was angry, he went into a deep silence, totally removing my access to him. Sometimes this lasted a few hours. Sometimes it was a few days. Finally, it was the silence that I could not walk across. I reacted by trying to avoid the silences, so I often did not approach subjects about which we might differ.

It would take me decades to realize that, just as I couldn't penetrate his silence, he didn't have the capacity to express his emotions in the way I wanted him to do.

I was taking wing with language: responding to the poets Dickinson, Whitman, Williams, Moore, Frost, and others. I wrote down what I could not express otherwise. On the page, I recognized the differences between us. The blank white spaces between us that I could not fill.

I used words with the children, filling in the gaps. Tom's Nordic reserve allowed him no resolution or absolution through language.

With each Idaho trip, we crossed the Nevada desert. Sometimes, I drove across it and Tom flew to meet us. Eventually, I wrote about these crossings:

Crossing the Desert

Through the window, the soft rise
of hip and curve, the desert is
laid out before me like a plain
and naked woman. Freckled with sagebrush
endless and warm in any direction
from Winnemucca. The blue-gray line
leading me takes me to less
safe roads, unending compromise,
eye-shadow and mascara

Through tinted sun glasses, a flash
A flicker of silver—the last Indian
signal or an unidentified object.
Lithe ghosts pile up here
like discards at a dump
and stillness like sand
Or dust that once danced
to an all-night band

I cross with the windows rolled up
exceeding the speed limit
turning the radio up to loud
driving all night in search of sunrise.

By the road, bits of fur and bone
Pock-marks on the smooth surface
Jack-rabbits, blinded by the light monsters
whirling by, smashing without a glance.
(Build an underground tunnel. Hire an escort)

Protected by manifold, metal and glass
I get the idea, without the heat, cold, gritty sand.
Impressions fly by, retreat
Over the rise in the rear-view window.

At what point did words become so important to me? And why? I've been reading most of my life and writing much of the time as an adult. Words help me explain everything—feelings, the inner (and the outer) landscape. Words explained the inexplicable. I write to make sense of my life and to redeem it. A line, a paragraph, and I realize that I have written something that I had not known until this moment.

We had neighbors I never saw. All I noticed was their automatic garage door going up and down as they came or left. I had great fun writing about them—all made up, of course. Somewhere between fiction and nonfiction, the mind weaves a story: Here are just a couple of paragraphs:

There may be people there. I only know what I see. Who can say what is behind things? The regular rise and fall of the automatic garage door, turning off and on of electric lights, these are real. Stay with the face of things, I say. Keep out of trouble.

Like morning coffee, that garage door, picking itself up. I can't read the paper 'til it has opened and closed. When that electronic glow from the family room continues for hours, I give long lectures about the evils of television watching. He never listens.

I invented George, who lived in the house across the street. What fun!

Words energized my life.

I soon found writing to be therapy, solace, and comfort in all the parts of me that needed nourishment. The pieces came together, sometimes briefly, but with each stroke of the typewriter, later the computer, I could feel myself healing. Just as surely as one watches a scar heal, my soul settled in a calm place. My sins, if indeed all the things that troubled me could be called that, were forgiven.

I started writing on a computer at the same time as I was studying surrealism. The two acted together: run, they said, say whatever is inside, without judgment, without syntax, let the words heal you. Sometimes it didn't feel like me, but a light that danced in my fingers, freeing half-framed thoughts, inarticulate feelings, making me whole.

The idea that I was born in sin and would die and burn forever, unless I accepted salvation through Jesus Christ, seemed remote. My mind was free of those fears. A distant myth that troubled me no longer.

Chapter Twelve

Family growth and change

As writing became my best way of communicating and knowing myself, I wanted to do it as much as I could. I was also raising a family and maintaining our home. For a brief time, I worked part-time at the telephone company in Oakland. The experience I'd had earlier in Boise helped me get the job.

Most of the employees were African American. As I worked with them, I began to see life from their viewpoint, which varied with each person, but all were different from mine. I met Black mothers whose life intent was to keep their children away from negative situations. Many of their children were in Catholic schools, as the mothers felt some good influences might exist there and they felt safer than public schools.

I also volunteered for Friends Outside, an organization whose goals were to support people held in the county jail before they had been tried and also support their families. I saw a different side of the world. Visiting the county jail in Martinez, I talked to prisoners. We didn't talk about what crime they had been charged with. Usually, it was mundane requests—their dog needed tending to, or maybe they needed someone to make a call to a mother or sister.

Most of them were young men of color, not much older than my own children. My sons lived in a comfortable suburb, with supportive parents, excellent schools, and a safe community. The men I talked to were used to violence being played out on the streets where they lived. I began to realize how much harder it is to have a positive life future for those who don't have the supportive things my sons had. Being Black wasn't just a skin color—it was a way people, people with authority, often saw you.

Following is the poem I wrote about that experience:

Visiting the Martinez County Jail

I.
Before I enter the massive stone
Building, I hide jewelry and identity
Iron bars on the windows. Behind
Them men make catcalls
Or whistle. I am not
To reply.

Before I enter the door, I prove
Myself. Pass ID through a small
Opening, someone has checked
Fingerprints with the FBI.
I take the passport back,
Something private
Is gone. I enter
The massive stone.

I follow along the gray
Corridor through one, two,

Leaving the Faith of Our Fathers

Three steel doors, listen
To the open/shut clang.
Concrete floors, assigned
Cells, where men in orange jumpsuits
And eyes glazed in unhope
Eat limp, gray food from metal trays
When they are told and what.

I watch everything
And nothing
Inside the massive
Stone being.

II.
Letter for Lonnie

The deputies sneer
Tell dirty jokes loud, so I will hear
Tell me they stood burning
In the burning sun
While their friend was buried.
They tell me you are dangerous
I don't have to see
The cop-killer.

Curiosity, I suppose,
I don't know what to say
And you want to know why
I'm here, why anyone would be,
If I get paid. I am not
To ask you about the alleged
Crime. There is a book
Of rules and it is.

It is clear, I am not to get
Personally involved. I can feed
Your dog. I can call
Your sister.

A book of rules. You
Know only my first
Name. We come from
The same county and different countries.
On Monday you go to
Court in shackles. On Wednesday
We pass slivers, in the cubicle.

Slivers of family and "in my country":
The safest community in the Bay Area
                    The streets of Oakland
The price of grass
            The price of ass
                and grass

Books of rules. You know
Them like a lawyer and write
A parody of the California
Criminal Code. Laws for pimps.
I take it out though I am not supposed to
Reading it, I am offended,
It is degrading to women. You
Scoff, "What would you know?"

Once when I came your buddy told me
They shoved you down four flights
Of stairs. "He's hurt bad,
Needs help." Once when I didn't
Come, you asked: "Did your son's team

Leaving the Faith of Our Fathers

Win," as from that other
Country you might ask, "Is there morning
There?"

Something has gone
Wrong. That is all
I know. A link
Or a leg.

As for the words
You wanted from me, how
It all started
Here

There is a book of rules
I am not to get involved
When I pass San Quentin
Everyone is faceless, but you
Who listened
To your human connection

As to why I never
Wrote: finally, I suppose my
Insistence on the rules
    Dress modestly
    Wear no jewelry or makeup
    For the prisoner
        Bring nothing in
        Take nothing out

Lois Requist

III.
The Woman

Her world is a gray box
With a lid only they can open
And a small hole they talk through
When they want to

She could pretend to be a child's pet
Soft rags and food in the box
The child would carry it around
Stroke her, show her to everyone

She doesn't pretend anymore
Looking in the mirror, makeup and men
Are things she's given up

The women in the day room
Still talk of men
Curl each other's hair
Smoke
Deal cards
Until they rub
The Joker's smile away

Now the gray box
A world of its own
A universe without sun or the concept

Her fingers are thin slivers of ice
There is no heat inside her body
Cold, blue blood slips through
Like an icicle
Her skin has pockets of shadows

Leaving the Faith of Our Fathers

If there is anything she wants
She would be a ghost
Slip through the bars
To the welcoming night

She's unable to slip
Out of consciousness to somewhere
Morning comes when she wants it
Doors open
Bodies slip in and out of each other
White wisteria climbs a certain wall

She tires of all this
Pulls razor across waist
Screams split the air as pores
Split into half-moons
of blood like a bright Hawaiian Hibiscus

The deputy runs, takes the lid off
Efficient hands wipe the offending blood
Bandage wrists

Take her downstairs
To lights and voices
Of another hemisphere

She slips, slips, slips

IV.
I have not told
Everything. Travelers
Should be aware
Of language and cultural

Differences, especially so
In this massive state.

A passport is only
Good for certain
Sections. Go
Somewhere else, where
The sun is. If you
Have a choice, go.

Tony, our elder son, took a solo bicycle trip across the country in 1985, while he was going to college. "That wouldn't have been safe to do if I was another color," he recently said.

By the time I finished going to college in the early 80s, I had a bachelor's and a master's degree in English/Creative Writing. This was around the time our sons were finishing high school.

I wanted to get involved in politics in a productive way. This led me to join the League of Women Voters, which was a rich learning experience. The process of consensus building was especially good for me. The League had studied national defense and was preparing to adopt an updated position. A movement began to urge the national level of the League to study global security. We went to the national convention and lobbied for such a study. We lost, but it was a great experience.

I've loved the consensus process since I learned and practiced it with the League. It encourages everyone to listen respectfully to opinions with which they differ. I wish more people were exposed to it.

Our children were growing into young adults, taking on their own skin. When their father started talking about getting a computer, they got excited. The first Apple we bought required a tape recorder to save things on. Soon, Tony was writing a word processing program, and I practiced using it. I'd write something, then he would see if he could save it. Extension cords were strung all over the family room, and, if the dog walked through and pulled on one of them, we very likely lost something. Tony eventually built the program and sold it. With the proceeds, he bought his first car. He attended the University of California, Berkeley, studying computer science. This is the poem I wrote about him when he left.

The day my son left for college

I left you writing notes on the internal failures
Of a computer. In the field
The ground cracks, unplanned lines
Jag and curl on the path,
Under the dry grass
The dog runs happily along.

I am going back now
Sliding with you in the snow
Loading a broken bike. Fishing
In Idaho. Towns along the Snake River
In a fifties scene. Irrigation water.
"Let's have all the kids line up over
Here." We drive hundreds of miles
To reach California.

Today you are leaving. Here in this field, I am alone.
Sharp stalks of grass. Wind rustling. Remnants
Of a plastic toy. A scrap of wood.
Cars pass along Moraga Road
A biker on the trail below—
He's you on the Davis Double Century
Running out of water far from any town.

The dog sniffs every possibility
Expects me to proceed
Or go home
Not sit watering this dry field
Your car headed west
The basketball rolling with the curve

You are here
The grass becomes soft
Spring green blades caress my ankles
You are everywhere
In all the sizes you've outgrown

I am there
Putting the blood mark over the door

******

As I grew strong and assertive in my writing, Tom peaked in his career, perhaps having lost sight of what and where the top of the mountain was. At 49, he was dissatisfied with his career and not too happy with me. All that had been so clear—devotion to his career and family—became muddled.

"It was the commute as much as the job," he told me later.

It seemed as if he looked down one morning and saw how many other men were wearing the same shoes. What had been a comfort, a sort of solidarity with other businessmen, now seemed a trap they had all been lured into. Our lifestyle, based as it was on what we learned as children in the 40s and 50s, put both of us in separate places, on tracks that eventually led to our seeing the world in different ways.

What role did I play? Was I, with my ideas that blossomed out in every direction, the cause? Or was it that my constant push to know more, see more, write more, and be more, perhaps influenced him? The world wasn't as simple as it had seemed before the Vietnam War, the sexual revolution, the women's movement.

As I write this on a rainy day in April 2022, I realize the length of time it took for me to change beliefs and attitudes. I didn't have an epiphany that made me turn around and walk the other way. Listening, reading, and living, I altered one step at a time. Michener's book, The Source, which I mentioned earlier, and Joseph Campbell's series The Power of Myth, were early influences. Dozens of books followed. I learned goddesses were part of the Bible in earlier times, but monks in the Catholic Church removed such references. Might gave men power over women. It was often used in horrible and violent ways.

I had married a good man who wanted a simple life. I challenged and railed against him, going on about women's rights. Okay, he said, you have a point, they have a point, but do they have to carry it so far, make it so annoying? What is so bad about staying home and raising kids? "Choice," I said. What choice had he?

The company he worked for that once had been small had been sold, and then sold again, to one of America's largest corporations. There were so many bosses and directions. He was a model employee, who never cheated and took as good care of the company's money as he did his own. Worked hard and smart. Traveled and moved and did what they told him. Now, they were moving past or around or under or over him. Maybe going in a direction that he could not or did not want to go.

He had raised a family, worked hard for 25 years, both at the office and at home. The company's home office in San Francisco was where many people aspired to be. Always, there were more bosses, more floors above him. He hadn't been prepared for the politics of it all. Goals and purpose became vague; when he ran a profit center, he knew what to do. Make a profit.

All those years of doing his job, somewhere along the line, soured. He had a home in the suburbs, a good job, and a family. He was tired. Very, very tired. (The doctor noted "unusually high white counts" in his blood.) He climbed the ladder and all he saw were more ladders leading to what he no longer grasped.

What did it all come to? That had become unclear. What was the reward? While my responsibilities had become lighter—the children caused no problems during their teenage years—his seemed heavy. I had probably come to see the regular inflow of his paycheck as automatic.

Tom provided home, safety, and comfort for us. The children knew nothing else, though I had seen to it that the boys knew everyone did not live comfortably. Tom had done what was expected of him. Had bought the dream. Graduated from college. Served in the U.S. Army. A few years later, men were saying "Hell no! We won't go!" Protesters in the streets supported their disaffection for the Vietnam War. He enlisted in 1958 without question and served his time. That did not include active duty in a war zone. He had always been prepared to do what he was told.

Still, all his disillusion welled in him. For years, I said to him: "We need to talk." He came to dread hearing me say it. Dreading his dread, I did not say it until small differences magnified to large hostilities. We never did it very well. I always wanted him to help me learn to dance, perhaps to recreate that moment long ago when we danced and he said, "I love you," as his arms so wonderfully encircled me. But he had not wanted to dance after we were married, and we had not learned to enjoy it together. It must have felt to him, sometimes, that he did everything for me, and that it was never enough, so he grew resentful.

These feelings finally resulted in action, not words. That was his way. At 49, he quit his job.

"Fine, if you want to quit, go ahead. I can get a job. Philip is through high school," I said. "We can both work."

In the early months after Tom left his job, he was elated. We would have a real estate business together. We studied and passed the required state test, but by then he decided not to start the business.

Six months after Tom quit, I took a position as Executive Director with the Lafayette Chamber of Commerce. Suddenly, my picture was in the paper, not once, but frequently, when a new business opened, or a local event took place. When he went to a social event with me, he was the adjunct.

"Mr. Lois" someone dubbed him. My world expanded at the same time his contracted. He had not looked for a job in 25 years. It was not easy.

The switch fractured some image of the way he thought things "should" be. I never sought a career, but now I had a job, and he did not. The change almost broke our relationship—that and the pile of little resentments each of us carried from house to house and year to year, like a special vase that once belonged to a grandmother.

Chapter Thirteen

What do we Really Share?

In 2021, when I said to Ernie, my sister, that I would like to talk with her, she said, "I haven't agreed with you about anything in the last thirty years except the O.J. verdict." That struck deep. It made me think. What did we share?

Once, at her house, she introduced me to a man who had run for governor of Idaho. He'd legally changed his name to emphasize his political position.

He said, "I'm Pro Life."

I said, "I'm pro-choice."

"That's okay. We can still talk," he responded.

When I approached my sister in 2021, asking for a conversation, she seemed to feel there wasn't much to talk about. We were pretty clear on where each of us stood. When we talked, it was mostly about family.

That extended family, the ones we visited each summer in Idaho, consisted of my oldest brother, Harry and his wife, Gloria, and their four children. The children eventually attended Oral Roberts University. Sometime in the 90s, my brother and his wife moved to Northern Idaho. One son, Nathan, and his wife moved with them. They all became involved with a church group in Oregon. I've never known exactly what that group believed—asking would require listening to a very long speech—except that the man of the family is always in charge and you should have as many children as you can. They also saw Saturday as the Sabbath rather than Sunday and used the name "Yahweh" to refer to God.

Three of Harry's children produced, respectively, nine, seven, and five children. I think all were home-birthed and home-schooled. The family with nine children raised them in Northern Idaho; the seven were raised in the Boise Valley, and the five were raised in Oklahoma.

By 2022, many of these children were married and having children, so there was always family to talk about. I attended weddings, grew restless watching the bride being "given" from the father to the groom, like some possession. After one of the weddings, I wrote:

Who gives this woman?

Garlands of flowers, a beaming bride in white
Young women attend in turquoise
Waiting their turn
To be given away

Guests arrive in their finery
The men in serious clothes, dark suits

Who ever thought of giving a man away?
The idea is absurd

Leaving the Faith of Our Fathers

A man is no one's possession
He is whole within himself

She will
Do his wash, clean his house
Take him in, inside her body

A woman named Liberty
Given away by her parents to a man, the groom
With admonitions that he is in charge

My mind reels over the millions of women
bartered, traded, sold, or given away

But Liberty is happy
She has chosen the man she is given to

And all the people sing
And say congratulations

The parents are happy
The married couple are happy
The people are happy

From inside, I am outside
Saying no, no, no

It's time for the cake

******

Stan, my older brother, was the special target of our father's wrath throughout his childhood—taking his cuffing and belittling words. He couldn't wait to get away from home, so he got married right out of high school to a fourteen-year-old girl. When that marriage ended, he enlisted in the U.S. Army and went to Fort Lewis, Washington. He married another young girl, racing away on the freeway to consummate the marriage before her parents could stop them. I guess that made it legal.

When he completed his time in the Army, they returned to the Boise Valley, where they had four children. On our yearly trips to Idaho, my sons played with these children, as well as Harry's children. My mother loved seeing her ten grandchildren, serving them ice cream, holding them.

Stan's family led a chaotic life. For a time, they lived about a quarter mile away from our mother. Once, when I was staying at Mother's with my boys, the cousins from Stan's house asked if eight-year-old Tony and five-year-old Phil could stay at their house for the night. I said okay.

About eleven o'clock, Tony called me.

"I can't stay here," he said. He and his brother came back to Mother's. There had been angry shouting that scared him.

That marriage, though troubled, lasted through much of the four children's childhood. The oldest went to college and has had a good life. The other three have had trouble, particularly the youngest one, Steve.

At one point, Steve and his wife had five children in the house under five years old, which would be challenging for anyone. For these parents, it was beyond their capacity. In the years after he went to prison for child abuse, Steve lived in a house in front of his father's house. Between the two homes, Steve created a place for wrecked cars and parts, which eventually included a railroad car and every kind of junk imaginable. To me, the junkyard was symbolic of Steve's life. In 2022, shortly before I wrote this, he died in a motorcycle accident.

The next generations didn't go to the Kingdom Church in the Boise Valley, where Ernie was the pastor. She still primarily preached the "Israel message," about England and the United States being the lost tribes of Israel. The rest of the family were Christian, but they put the emphasis on different things. The family that grew up in the Boise Valley were taught that by serving other people they were serving God. Some of them went to China and smuggled Bibles across the border. They offered support to children who age out of the foster care system. They offer support to unwed mothers. They all oppose abortion.

While it feels invasive to talk about actual people in my family, I try to do it with compassion and understanding. People don't just turn out to be what they are; it all comes from somewhere.

When I try to answer my sister's question: what is there to talk about? I have to think about what we do share.

We share what our mother taught us: to be good, to be fair and honest in every situation, to be respectful and kind. Being good means more than just following the rules. It means being good to everyone we encounter, being fair and honest in all interactions. These are the basis of what Mother taught us, by example more than by preaching. This is what we still share. We may have gotten some of this from the church, I'm not sure.

What comes back to me, now in my eighties, is the calm and measured way Mother approached every demand her children and her husband made. How she considered what should be done, always with the good of us all in her mind and heart.

This was the same woman who brought me into the Kingdom Church. At that time, when I was a child, I don't remember hearing anything about our being better than anyone else. She thought we were to be a servant nation to the rest of the world, to bring them to God.

At that time, we didn't know anything about other faiths—the Christian churches we grew up with were the only thing I knew. Eventually, I would meet Buddhists, and people from many faiths. I also visited India and China. In India, I saw temples—built hundreds or thousands of years ago. I saw a different faith being lived out and how it impacted the culture. It was the culture, really.

In time, I learned more about how Europeans colonized the rest of the world for centuries, with both economic and religious aims. Whole civilizations were destroyed. In some South American countries, births and deaths were recorded by the Catholic Church. If you weren't part of the church, there was no record of you.

In the United States Constitution, full rights were given to white men with property. Women had to fight until 1920 to get the vote. Treaties negotiated with the American Indians were tossed out the window when they conflicted with the new country's desires. We've all heard of the "Trail of Tears." Then, there's slavery. No wonder many white men are angry. They've had centuries of living and believing that they should be in charge of everything. Now all these women and people of color are challenging that. The move is on to restrict women again.

Right now, when I think about my mother and the rest of my family, I start to say, it's complicated. Perhaps that is why we've been able to have good relationships despite our differences. Recognizing the good in people you don't agree with is the beginning of respect.

In all these years, when I'm with my siblings, the bond we grew up with is still there. The basics of what Mother taught us about goodness still exist.

******

In August of 1987, I told Tom I was moving out. He cried, something I'd never seen him do. In the next few months, we would meet and talk over everything that had happened in our years together. We talked more than we ever had, talked to our limit of understanding.

It would be easy to say I married the wrong person, but how can I say that when I remember all the good times, or look at my sons, or think about how Tom made us all laugh? When the silence was pushed back, we enjoyed each other, enjoyed being a family. This imperfect union contained joy, love, and laughter. He took care of us. Now, in 2022, I understand at what cost.

There was enough fault to go around. Both of us fell short, or made an incorrect estimate, in that long ago when physical attraction overrode more mundane considerations.

He provided for and protected me. I stepped out from under that umbrella, and said, "Thank you, but I must be able to stand on my own."

He still wanted me, still needed my body to open and hold him. This is my body broken and spilling for you. Take it as my expression, as I have no voice. No verbal sound that will bring us together.

Briefly, sporadically, that conjunction brought unity. Sometimes, for me, this more-than-sexual union forged all the connections in a split second—the spirit, mind, and body sharing one purpose, one peace.

While we were separated, Phil, who was attending the University of California, Santa Barbara, asked us to go there together. We could do that. Always civil toward one another, we didn't yell or shout. Phil perhaps felt spending time together might help us get back together.

We drove south on Highway 101 towards Santa Barbara.

Out the window, I noticed a small, 1940s wood-frame house, like the one I grew up in and around. Idly, it occurred to me that life would be simpler in that house and that town. Still, I could not live there. The rooms were too square, the windows too narrow. My skin would prickle in the hot, stuffy air. I would develop a rash. I needed more outside inside.

I imagined—I like imagining and I write these conjectures down—that the gray-green chairs are overstuffed. The big arms of the chairs are covered with off-white, lace doilies—needlework that someone's grandmother had labored over, straining, leaning forward, as the light and her eyesight failed.

"Who are you writing to?" Tom asked.

I read aloud what I had written.

Without comment, he said: "Did you write a thank you note to my mother and brother?"

"No," I wanted to scream, "don't you understand the difference between 'writing' and writing thank you notes?"

Tom had the radio on, listening to the Dodgers. I was a Dodgers fan, out of some old loyalty—when I was a kid, they were in Brooklyn—but I did not really listen.

"You can change the station if you want," he said, knowing that I don't like hearing ball games all the time; still, he did not turn it off himself.

"No. It leaves my brain free for other things."

He turned the radio off.

When I was comfortable, Tom was too warm. When he was comfortable, I was cold.

I returned to my writing—seeing in my mind the little house we had passed a few miles back. A man comes in, sits in "his" chair, belching as he drinks beer and watches TV. His clothes are dusted with soil. I couldn't live there.

Tom switched the radio on. I switched the writing off, needing silence.

"I'm trying to break my habit of feeling I have to write at the computer, when no one else is around."

"You're writing for your own amusement?"

"No," I said, feeling that phrase as an old disappointment. "I'm just trying to write, without thinking of an audience, or will it sell, or who will read it."

That year it rained early then stopped. The hills were green. On the farms, laborers moved down the rows with hoes, weeding. Highway 101 cuts through the California farmland like a ribbon that doesn't match, a barrier, something foreign and fixed.

Those people who live near 101, like the woman in the gray-green house (no, the sofa was gray-green, but the feeling of gray green pervades the place), keep their windows closed against the sound. The shades are drawn to keep out all those who hurry by. People do not slow down here.

That woman buys practical clothes, tennis shoes at the supermarket, forty miles south in Paso Robles. Her family goes there occasionally. Inside the house is her life. Regular. The children go to school. He plows the field and drinks when he can.

This is fiction. I take pleasure in molding these people in this house, in the small town along Highway 101.

That other woman watches a couple of the soaps while her husband is gone and talks with a friend. She rarely looks outside to where everything is green, and the dirt is soft and moist and brown and fertile. I use all those "ands" because I like to, and the land deserves it, deserves to be spread out, sifted through, handled.

The dirt tracks, blows and sifts inward, settling on every surface. Mostly that woman has given up dusting, her rag unequal to the constant deluge. He brings it in, carrying pockets of it in the crevices of his body. Sometimes, after they have had sex, hurried and rough because that's the way he wants it, she finds the gritty brown in the crevices of her body. She takes a shower.

"No, it's not for my own amusement," I said to Tom. "Well, I like it, of course, but...take playing the piano. I don't play well, but I enjoy playing. I know I'll never be really good at it. I play the piano for my own amusement."

"Oh," Tom responded and set his lips.

A marriage counselor told us that every time a couple comes to see him, each is bringing the other for correction.

I wrote. While the woman takes a shower, she thinks. It is all so different on the soaps. Those people never get dirty. She wonders sometimes what it is like for him. A triumph?

Dressing, she dreams that someday she will go somewhere south and sexy on 101. She will sit on a terrace having a margarita.

******

All the time I lived in the apartment, I tried to figure out whether it was simpler, living alone, only being responsible for one person.

That autumn, while on my own, I drove all over the West. While still working at the Chamber of Commerce, I took a bit of time off. Driving, I did not even turn the radio on in the car. I crossed parts of Idaho and all of Oregon, while the trees changed from what was always called those "glorious" colors of fall, dropping their leaves, turning black and stark. In Idaho, most of the trees were next to farmhouses, often in tall, thin lines, protecting the houses from the wind.

I imagined a sheltered figure going beyond the protection to exposure, flying or falling...which is it...without protection...is it free-falling, or just free?

In the season of our separation, everything seemed to be in a state of decay and dissolution. While I drove through the western states, trying to find direction, the generation that raised my generation was dying.

The separation was a sort of death: no one else knew all that stuff about my family and his family and that the differences between living in Idaho and California were, for us, more significant than state lines and climate.

Their deaths came in rapid succession. The plural pronoun "their" may be wrong for events so singular, so personal. Death cannot be shared.

"The fever called living is over at last," according to Poe.

That fall and winter there were so many.

Aunt Alice, the wife of my father's brother, was 94, had raised flowers, canned peaches and plums, and, as a proud German, had taken care of her own house until near the end. Years before, on a visit to Idaho, I admired her irises. When I returned to California, a package of iris bulbs arrived, packed in dirt, with a handwritten note carrying instructions for planting and care. I followed the guide but never separated them as often as Aunt Alice had instructed. They had to adjust to the California climate, but the irises still bloomed all over the backyard.

Right after Alice died, Uncle Otis, the husband of my mother's sister, died. I had known him all my life. I returned to Idaho for the funeral. My brothers, sister, and cousins were there. I remembered when we were kids, playing tag and hide-n-seek on warm summer nights in Idaho, while the grown-ups sat on the porch or around the picnic table.

Uncle Otis's son, Wayne, was married with children when he announced he was gay. After the divorce, he moved back to the Boise Valley. His sister and brother, as well as two of my brothers, would have nothing to do with him. My sister did. She showed him kindness and compassion until he died of AIDS. When Wayne came to his father's funeral, he brought his Black lover.

I thought of way back when we were kids. How innocent we had all been. How scarred we all were now from our own and others' failings. How triumphs are pulled, tugged, and forced from grit and reality.

Chapter Fourteen

Resolution and Illness

After several months, I moved back home. We decided to try it again. Almost a quarter of a century of a "good marriage" was hard to put aside.

I was putting the books I had taken back on the shelves. Tom wandered into the room. It was hard for me to handle books, because I wanted to sit down and read each one.

"I was interested to see what books you left," Tom said, watching me from a chair. "You left the Fix-It-Yourself Manual and the Bible."

"You were covered in any case."

"Now, I won't be able to find anything."

"The next time you want to read Robert Frost let me know. I'll find him for you."

"I like books. Not that I read many of them. I just like having them around," he said.

"Does it make you feel more knowledgeable, just having them here? Maybe you pick up something just by being in the room with these volumes? Soon you'll know all of these poems.

I've been meaning to read this *Outline of History* ever since I was 20. Figured then I would understand everything."

Earlier, when I had packed, I hadn't thought about what books to leave, but what I needed to take. I had to have Adrienne Rich's "The Dream of a Common Language," another book by a woman whose opening sentence was "a whole new language is a temptation. "W.H. Auden's *Horae Canonicae*, or the Canonical Hours, which opened a new way of thinking for me. An ordinary day in which a fallen world is offered redemption.

Fallen. That's the crux of the matter. I suppose theologians have many ways to explain the fall. Imperfect, no doubt we are. If we are what we are by way of evolution, there has to be a big dose of self-preservation in us. Evolution seems a more natural way to explain us and all our characteristics than does the eating of an apple by Eve. Millions of people have been told they are sinners and they accept it as fact. Why don't I? I recognize good and bad instincts in myself, but nothing so bad as to warrant burning in hell forever. No way.

Something about a tortured Edgar Allan Poe fascinated me and, in quite another way, a tortured Virginia Woolf.

Again, another morning, I tried to return to writing. Tom came in: "Would you like coffee?" He set a steamy mug down. Later, he crept in quietly to pick up the cup and refill it.

"You are too kind," I smiled.

"I need support for my 80-foot radio tower," he said. He did. From both me and the neighbors.

One morning, I closed all the doors to the computer room, even though I liked them open. It seemed like ideas flowed more easily. Somewhere a toilet flushed. A door closed. Footsteps pounded through the house. The coffee. The animals. The newspaper. I started sneezing. It was a conspiracy. All I wanted was silence. Again, a door.

"Could you wait to run the sprinkler lines until I'm through writing?"

I was tempted by "a whole new language." Would that help? I knew which button to press on the computer to erase what would not do, but what button should I press to get out the important stuff?

"Do you remember my original plan for this room?" Tom said while sitting in the room with the bookshelves he had built.

"No," I replied. We both failed each other in certain and significant ways.

"I wanted to put a shelf all the way around the room. Just one foot down from the ceiling. That would have held a lot of books and would look nice."

"Yes, but...you couldn't reach those books. What is the point of having books you can't reach? The shelf becomes a dust catcher."

"How often do you read those books? When you want them, stand on a chair."

When Tom and I decided to get back together, we took a short cruise to celebrate. However, this wasn't a time for celebration. Two calls to the ship told us that Tom's father was in serious condition. When we left the ship, we returned to Idaho.

In the hospital, I tried to talk to my father-in-law about simple things. His grandchildren. The fishing trips. The card games. We had always been polite to each other, but left together in a room, with no one else, we had nothing to say.

"Do not go gentle into that good night, / Old age should burn and rave at close of day..." Dylan Thomas wrote.

And rave is what my father-in-law did. He tore at the intravenous tubes and catheter and the restraints that held him tied to the bed. Sneaking a knife from the dinner tray, he jabbed at the covers, at anything he could touch. His arms were black and blue from the struggle.

When my sister visited him, he said: "Get the scissors. Get the car. Pay the bill. Let's get out of here."

Road conditions were hazardous when we returned two weeks later for Tom's father's funeral. The highway pavement in the corner of Oregon through which we drove had a snow floor. Driving snow and wind pushed against the vehicle. The big rigs that passed almost blew our car off the map, into a white, swirling world. Thermometers hung at around zero in Boise. The landscape was white and black. The trees formed epitaphs on the winter sky. People bundled up, stoked the fire, protecting themselves from the cold.

Recent months had brought several deaths in the older generation of my family. It was perhaps a benevolent spirit that diminished with these deaths: people who cared about us. There are never too many. Two I had known all my life and, perhaps, still saw me in an innocent light. Two others, who, perhaps, never knew me, or perhaps were as aware as I was of our inability to understand each other.

My marriage, too, was a fragile thing.

It served no purpose to think of whether we were "meant" for each other in the beginning. In the years together, we had become "one flesh." The pain of splitting was enormous, and only seemed warranted by major flaws, not many small differences.

Still, Aunt Alice's iris bulbs, or anyone's for that matter, only grew so long in that thick cluster beneath the ground. To survive, they had to be dug up, pulled apart, and started again.

When we left Idaho to return to California, we drove two cars, taking one that had belonged to my in-laws. The police stopped both of us for speeding, shortly before we reached Winnemucca. A little later, over lunch at a Western style casino and cafe, we commiserated over the tickets, the speed trap.

"It's not worth fighting it," we said at the same time. "We'll send a check."

It was the kind of story we would tell later, to family and friends.

"He was coming the other way. He was behind a big truck. They love to bag Californians."

******

The woman I'd imagined in the house off Highway 101 is who I thought I would be, had I allowed my life to be simpler. At least a part of me will always be in a small, rectangular house in the middle of farm country.

Still, another part wants to go beyond the protection, beyond the safe arms, to look as far in either direction as eye and the land and mind allow. I use all those "ands" because I like them. That idea needs space and expansion.

Book by book, page by page, word by word, I've moved away from the faith of our fathers to a broader, more open, spacious, and free world. It had to be! I couldn't be locked in, running up against one rule after another.

******

On my 50th birthday, Tony and his wife, Carrie, stopped in around six. Tony wanted to take me for an ice cream sundae. When we returned, it was to a surprise party. Tom had kept the food at our neighbors' and directed the guests to park on side streets. I was surprised. This gesture was so uncharacteristic. I wasn't dressed for a party, so my appearance bothered me all evening.

The next day, Tom told me he didn't feel well and hadn't for a while. He'd put off going to the doctor until after the party. We went to the doctor's office the next week.

The diagnosis was swift: cancer of the lymph glands in Stage Four, an advanced stage. I did not know the word—lymphoma. It sounded lumpy, awkward, and difficult to get a handle on. Lymph is a colorless fluid from tissues or organs of the body, containing white blood cells. A lymph node is a small mass of tissue where lymph is purified. He had a swelling in his groin—in a lymph node, the cells meant to save the body from infections. What happens when the nodes turn on you?

Coming home, I was so tired. I felt drugged. I stumbled walking through the house.

"I don't want you to hover over me," he said. "I can't stand that."

"If or when you do want or need me to do something for you, tell me," I responded.

After that, we both slept, blotting out what we had just learned, and what would come next.

Chemotherapy began as soon as it could be scheduled.

As the earth turned green outside, we settled in with this new reality.

In five months, chemo had reduced the cancer to a low level.

The doctor said, "If there is anything you want to do, do it."

Stationed in Darmstadt, Germany, in 1960, Tom had taken military "hops" around the continent. He wanted to show me Copenhagen, Paris, and some places in Germany. I wanted to touch some literary and historical ground in England. We flew to London.

I turn to pictures and papers of that time. We were on British Airways flight #286, row 43, arrival date—October 2, 1989. Tom, in a red shirt and gray sweater, posed in front of a small garden in London. Always photogenic, he could turn on a smile for the camera no matter what his real mood was, though I believe he was happy there, as much as one can be with cancer always lurking nearby. A smiling Tom rode down the Thames, while bridges and other sites were pointed out.

In some ways, the diagnosis was freeing—living in the moment became real, not just an idea. Always fiscally cautious, he would have said we couldn't afford to go to Europe until he got the cancer diagnosis.

He took my picture at the Tower of London, where I tried to think what it was like for those people who spent their last moments alive there. How limited we are by our concepts of time and existence. Yesterday is over, but not quite.

It was cold and blustery when we drove to Stonehenge. We had to ask directions. I marveled that there was none of the hype that would surround such a place in America. Then, to a comfortable bed-and-breakfast just outside Bath. We passed small, flower-filled back yards.

My genetic roots are English, and growing up with Bronte, Austen, Hardy, Shakespeare, and others, my literary roots are there as well. I felt a sense of returning to my homeland.

Hamburg, Cologne, the memories flew past, and that wonderful ride on the Rhine through centuries of living and warring. See the castle! On the boat, a family celebration took place while the world went by—the toasts as loud as if no one else were in the room. Bacharach on the Rhine—where everything was a scene from yesterday and before. Rudesheim and Assmanhausen are blends of original and refurbished, designed for tourists.

We visited the Army base at Darmstadt where Tom was stationed in 1960. A little piece of America. A different person now, did he look about for shadows of his former self? He would laugh at that.

Late at night, we checked into a hotel in Durbach. The young woman at the desk was friendly, but no one else spoke or smiled at us. Returning from dinner, the clerk said to us,

"There was an earthquake in San Francisco!" We ran to our room and got right through to Tony and found that he was okay and things were fine, if a bit, well, unsettled. When we went back to the bar, everyone was solicitous: "Is your family all right?"

Tom ate bratwurst in Freiburg, and admired the quaint architecture, immersed himself in a bubble bath so I could just see his head. I remembered laughing and drinking beer all over Germany, cuddling. Just the two of us then. Everything was okay. Almost.

On the next page, we were in Dijon, France, where he looked confused but soon grew to appreciate the food there. The catacombs beneath the church. I smiled and ate lunch at a picnic table in the countryside, walking the grounds of the chateau at Fontainebleau and then on to Versailles, and finally Paris. So many smiling pictures. The moment was working.

I was getting my first taste of other countries, similar cultures, but different. And the history! It's everywhere and feels alive. Europe is a museum of hundreds of years before there was a United States of America.

Better or worse? Different. Does America have to be the greatest place on earth for everything? Where does this competition come from? I enjoy the differences. Having lived my whole life in the western part of the United States, I notice cultural differences within my own country.

We like to think we are the most free, here in America. It's much more nuanced than that. Now, in 2023, I'm more comfortable out and about in European cities than I am in many places in my country. So many more guns here!

I've walked away from the narrow views I was taught as a child. And it's wonderful!

In early 1990, Tom did not look or act sick. Lymphoma doesn't show on the outside, but his energy level was affected. He grew tired frequently. Still, we lived normally. I even suggested he might want to look for a job. We had some hope. A cure could be found. We had today. I continued to work at the Chamber of Commerce.

He went through the year without treatment, though bone marrow tests showed the disease still present. We began planning another trip. While I was at the office, he read travel books, went to consulates of various countries in San Francisco, and planned our itinerary.

In the fall, we traveled to London. At Windsor Castle, I walked the walls while he sat in the courtyard. The royals and the churches always have the best real estate.

Tom had taken up an old interest—amateur radio. In Christchurch, we visited two couples. The men were radio operators that he had talked to regularly. We had high tea, which of course has more food than most meals do at home. The women did not talk much. One was serving, the other seemed content to listen. I was neither.

While the men looked at radio equipment, I took a walk in the woods nearby.

"We worried about you. Someone was murdered in those woods," the woman said when I returned.

We drove west through villages, past thatched-roof houses, and visited Thomas Hardy's cottage, buried deep in the woods, surrounded by a voluptuous garden. I loved being there, reading his poem on the wall, remembering the richness of his novels.

We headed towards Cornwall. I picked up a novel about the War of the Roses and sank into the past. Cornwall lends itself to this—its remoteness, the sheep, rocks, hedgerows, and moors. Then there's Tintagel with its old stone post office from the 14th century and some kind of deviled chocolate cake that

I would sell my soul for. Not noted for culinary skills, the English still have a few foods they do very well.

Travel opened the world to us and we shared the discovery. I look at the pages and want to go back. Covered in charm and flowers, canals and castles, filled with pubs and tea shops, that is the English countryside.

We went north, back and forth along the Welsh/English border, staying and taking a walking tour in Chester, led by a man whose family has lived there for a thousand years.

"'Ring Around the Rosie' was started here during the Black Plague." He showed us ruins from the Roman invasion.

Wales is said to have more sheep than people. I would not dispute it. I liked these hilly, isolated places, with the occasional village, the stonework. Wordsworth's Cottage in the Lake Country and Haworth, where the Brontes lived. We walked the moors.

An overnight freighter took us to the islands of Jersey and Guernsey off the coast of France. We drove the Normandy coast, saw the bunkers, the cemeteries, all the reminders of violence, death, and victory. Tom had watched endless World War II movies. He was really into this part.

These years passed in suspended animation, like flying at 35,000 feet when the flight is smooth and you have been on board for hours, as if there were nothing but the two of us simply moving through the atmosphere without direction or a scheduled landing time.

He never wanted to come home from these trips.

Regular check-ins with the doctor continued.

A writer friend said, "Are you keeping a journal?"

I began one.

Chapter Fifteen

Living with An Uninvited Guest

Living with cancer in the house is like having an unwanted guest, who invades every space, touches everything, points out your every weakness and never cleans up.

Tom and I shared a desire to get rid of the uninvited guest. Like knowing the roof might cave in at any moment, we huddled together against a force we couldn't control. Oh, we would always be very different. He would always want to watch the ball games or talk with his ham radio buddies; I would always want to slip away and search for a hidden word, a combination of phrases or paragraphs that would illuminate my world.

We'd taken some hits. A separation, and then the cancer. *(Was there a connection? I would always wonder.)* Our stable world was shaking. I never for a minute forgot the cancer that grew in our house, in his body. He tried to forget. He said he would follow the doctor's orders. Beyond that, he would live his life. The trips to Europe began, outposts really, almost like we could leave reality and that unwelcome guest at home.

I spoke to the doctor when Tom wasn't around, asking him about our future.

"Tom has many months of quality time," he said.

"Will he get to a place when he needs lots of care?"

"Yes. Three to five years. He is young and strong."

We attended one class of an eight-session wellness group. In high school, Tom was named the class clown. That day, with the group, he joked, smiled, and was kind and friendly to everyone.

Outside, he said, "I don't want to go back."

Friends and family wanted to help us find a cure, to show their caring. Perhaps, some combination of the right foods, thoughts, and activities would defeat the cancer. One suggested a clinic in San Diego, but Tom would have to stop smoking, drinking, and eating meat. People told him to clear the mind and body of impurities. Laugh. Hold a positive thought. My mother sent a book about conquering cancer through prayer.

He took the advice of his doctor. Otherwise, he did what he wanted, ate huge slabs of red meat, lots of butter, and drank buttermilk. Smoked.

I said to him: "I've decided not to nag you to death."

We disagreed as vociferously as ever, but now out loud. We shared global and domestic happenings—the 1989 fall of the Berlin Wall and the cat's idiosyncrasies.

I complained about his smoking. He was considerate of other people, didn't smoke in their house, car, or office. At home, he smoked everywhere. In bed. Incessantly in the radio room.

When I came home from work, the smell of smoke reached me first, before we greeted each other. In the car, stale smoke was the first thing I noticed. I heard about the effects of second-hand smoke and moved a little farther away from his cigarette. From him.

I read the book on conquering cancer through prayer. "Read it, or read it with me," I said. I put it on the coffee table, beside the bed, in all the obvious places. He never opened it.

Why did I want him to read it? Did some part of me still believe or at least want to? Did I want something outside myself that might save us? I saw it as a positive and active thing he (we) could do. A little less just taking it as it comes. Putting up some resistance. Taking an active role in what this disease does inside his body. Opening himself to possibilities. As far as I know, he never sought God, not before the illness or after.

"Sierra Kilo Sierra" was his call name on the ham radio, and he repeated it many times each day. It is what he can do. One room of the house had the component parts—receivers, transmitters, stuff I couldn't identify, and his computer. I had a computer in another room. Much of the time, we were in separate places.

He talked to people all over the world. Some became friends. Oshi from Japan visited. Tom had a local circle of buddies he had built around this hobby.

A friend brought over a videotape, a segment of the "Today" show about diphtheria fusion toxin, an experimental treatment. When treated with it, two lymphoma patients made excellent improvement, maybe even cured.

Tom applied and was approved for disability. This made him eligible for Medicare within a year and made it possible for me to leave my job, which I had wanted to do for some time.

We both loved going to Europe, so we planned another trip there. I kept a journal; some of it was used for newspaper articles in the local paper, the Contra Costa Sun.

In October 1991, we arrived in Amsterdam. First thing we did was visit Anne Frank's hiding place, which was just around the corner from our hotel. Soon, we took the train to Strasbourg, France, and then Heidelberg, Germany, loving the days, overusing words like quaint and charming. Mark Twain and his family lived in Heidelberg for a time. Tom loved eating Weinerschnitzel and bratwurst.

We met Tony and Carrie in Munich. I saw them walking into the hotel and I loved them for being there, bringing their youth, optimism and easy smiles. We traveled to castles, through Austria and into Switzerland. Staying in a little village near St. Moritz, we watched the cows walk through town, the bells on their necks ringing.

We returned home, settled into our routines. Our guest was still there. Never picked up the mail or took down the cobwebs.

I left my job at the Lafayette Chamber of Commerce in February of 1992. We drove to Idaho.

"No one said anything," Tom remarked when we left my mother's house. He repeated those words often. Cancer was the central factor in his life. If it was acknowledged, then conversation could move to weather, football, politics or whatever. Otherwise, that fact ballooned in his mind, blocking other words.

Does everyone want to share what is happening when the body's systems fail, when something inside turns ugly?

"Progression" is the term the medical reports use, referring to the direction of the disease, not the condition of the patient.

When we returned home, he was up all hours of the night and slept whenever he could.

"I sold a story to *Oh! Idaho*," I said, opening the mail.

"Oh, good," he responded.

"It won't be published until 1993."

"I might not be around then," Tom said.

By May the doctor said he needed to treat the disease more aggressively, so Tom would need to stay in the hospital at the beginning. With this treatment, he would lose all his hair.

Tom's aunts—his mother's sisters—Marg and Blanche, were coming from Idaho. The whole house needed cleaning. I tried to write, so the words inside me would survive, so that when I sat down, they would emerge. I would see the light coming in the window, the green, the light.

It is 2022. As I put up Christmas decorations, I notice the handmade ones from Blanche. One is made from an eggshell. She cut an oval in the shell and set a scene of Santa and a reindeer inside and put beading around the cut edge.

I hang every piece she made every Christmas, remembering her, thinking of her hands touching what I now handle. Most of them are needlework, petit point. Some are dated: 1979. 1982.

I think of Marg and the thick glasses she always wore. She had had cataract surgery in the 50s and stayed in the hospital for ten days. Ever after she wore very thick lenses.

Threads. Strings of connections that run through our lives. Blanche, who was a hairdresser most of her life, gave us these pieces of herself, just as I write words to survive. Wanting something to stick after we are gone.

I need to tell you how I got from there to here—dropped the Christian faith but found satisfaction in following my instincts, not being in constant conflict. I found a life worth living.

Aunt Blanche and Marg visited. Tom's oldest and closest relatives who were still alive, they had known him and been around him his entire life. Since neither one of them had children, they enjoyed Tom and his cousins, Neil and Ann, when they were growing up, often taking them on excursions.

Now, they laugh together over the rented motorboat at Payette Lakes that lost its motor. Tom and Neil had to row them back to shore, while Ann said, "Isn't this fun?"

It was comforting to have them there. They sat in the backyard and talked with Tom, wanting to do this, not having some other urgent place to go, not eager to go anywhere. This was what they came for.

At night, when the others had gone to bed, Blanche and I talked. She told me about when her husband, Herb, died.

"Once, I was so tired. I had just gotten something for him, when he rang the bell again. I asked what he wanted. He said, 'Nothing, it's the only thing in this world I can do—ring this bell.'"

Tom got a good report from the doctor. The new chemo was working. As evidence, he lost eight pounds, which were mostly infected lymph nodes. He was told he might only have to take six treatments.

He lost his hair. Nothing about his illness had shown before. Each day, he showed me handfuls of hair. He placed a sign on the front door: "Danger, falling hair."

Another report told us there was minimum disease residual after the effect of three treatments. The hope was, with three more, he would be in remission.

"It's the best news I've had in three and a half years," Tom said.

What did we do then? Our uninvited guest left for a few days, planning on returning, I supposed, but when?

The story changed by January 1993.

"It's worse," the doctor announced.

"It is?"

"Yes. That's what it says. I'm gonna look at the CAT scan myself, but it says it's worsening."

"You mean the chemotherapy didn't work?"

He continued to look at all the records, then sat down.

"The chemo worked to some extent, but the lymph nodes in the abdomen are worse than they were in August. We could use radiation, but it wouldn't do anything for the rest, in other areas."

He started talking about an antibody type of treatment, done by Dr. Leahy at Stanford. It worked well on a wealthy man, who donated quite a bit to make the treatment possible for other people. No side effects. It was experimental, though. Not much of a track record.

We were sober after the report, discussing the trip to Europe we hoped to take in October. We also discussed this with the doctor, who said, "Wait a couple of months if you don't have to decide earlier."

******

Our 30th anniversary was in February of that year. We went with our children to San Francisco to celebrate.

After dinner, Tom said, "How about an Irish coffee at the Buena Vista?" We piled in the car and headed that way. Where is it? A few wrong turns. Finally, we were there. Saturday night at 11 o'clock, it was so packed, it didn't look as if we could get in. Tom muscled his way in, gave the order to the waitress. A fight began in the middle of the crowd. I couldn't see much. As Tom pushed his way forward, he told me to follow. I did for a minute, then tapped him on the shoulder.

"I'm staying here. I'm not going into that." Then I turned to our kids and said, "I don't know if it's a good idea to be with someone who thinks he has a short life span."

Chapter Sixteen

Escaping with Travel: Finally, No Escape

Tom's health continued to decline as the disease progressed. So ironic these terms! By 1993, he wasn't nearly as strong as a couple of years before. While we wanted to return to Europe, we knew it needed to be different, with more time and space for Tom to rest. I had an acquaintance, a woman I worked with, who had a place in a little village—Istrago, Italy—that she was willing to rent to us, so we arranged to do that. I continued to keep a journal and published accounts of our trip when we returned.

We were in Vienna in August 1993. Leaving there, we had a leisurely day on an uncrowded boat along the Danube. Tom got excited as we began going through the locks. He watched the process from the upper level of the boat. After lunch, we sat on the deck together, and I kept dozing off. We talked, laughed, and compared this to our trip on the Rhine.

At Melk, we had reservations "beneath the abbey." We surveyed the town, sat down for a beer. I couldn't sit still. All the little stores were open. We bought soap and water. Ate at the Rathskeller. Tom fell asleep early. A heavy rain started. I bought a fan that Tom described as "cheap and tiny." It was.

He spoke of it again the last Friday night of his life. Tony didn't understand what he was saying, thought he was talking about milk.

"No, Melk. He's talking about the fan I bought in Melk."

In Salzburg, we learned the city's name was derived from salt when it was as valuable as gold. We toured the fortress by way of the funicular. Six hundred years in the building, starting in 1077 AD. Seventeen archbishops led the construction—and everything else, dominating the spiritual and political landscape until Napoleon defeated them.

To be in trouble with the law was to also have trouble with the church, and to question the teachings or the actions of the church could cause punishment by the state. The two were one.

We were shown the instruments of torture, told how the iron vest was heated white hot before it was put on the victim.

"Is there a record of how many people were tortured? Just a few?"

"Thousands were, and it continued until 200 years ago."

The guide showed us the mark made on a marble column by a cannonball shot in the revolt of 1525, where the peasants shot from the public square, a quarter mile away, at the central wooden beam in the fortress, where the archbishops lived. They lived on top of the building with "stars" made of pure gold above their heads. They slept near God.

People were accused of witchcraft or of being werewolves during medieval days. For example, from 1675 to 1690, 100 people were tortured and killed for such charges. Some of them were children.

Leaving the Faith of Our Fathers

This was one of many experiences I've had, through years of reading and traveling, of corruption in the church, with the common folk suffering from the dominance of the "holy" men. I didn't give up on the Christian faith because of one thing, but many. So many books I read, and history. Traveling in Europe brought historical events to life, to reality.

Enroute to Istrago, Italy, from Salzburg, we took in the lush mountains dotted with alpine cabins, ski slopes, and villages. Istrago is a village of 600 in Northern Italy, between Trieste and Venice.

Arriving midafternoon, we found the house we were renting but didn't know how to find Michelle—the caretaker we were to meet. Parking the car, we walked into the nearest ristorante, asked for Michelle. Immediately everyone was involved in where is Michelle, and who were we?

"Come with me," a man said. We followed. We walked a block or two, and he knocked on a door. Michelle answered. Introductions were made all around. They didn't speak English, we didn't speak Italian, but everyone tried and laughed. Michelle offered "vino," and who were we to say no? She brough out a local white wine. Tom held up his glass and said, "Cheers." Everyone joined in with "salud." Then she offered Belgian chocolate and I took one. I had to be a good guest. You don't want to start off on the wrong foot.

An hour or so later, after many laughs and an offer of a locally made kirsch—which was 90 proof. I turned it down, while Tom took a sip—Michelle guided us to where we were to stay in an immaculate, three-story home. Our apartment was on the second floor and contained a bedroom, bath, entryway, living room, and kitchen with a balcony. It was not luxurious, but sparsely furnished, with a dull, gray feeling. Michelle promised to be back at eight o'clock to take us to the local celebration, a festival of some kind, we didn't know what, but they said we should not eat before we went.

Tom took a nap.

That evening, we had excellent pasta. Wine was passed around the table. Everyone talked at once, it seemed. We met an English family who became our translators while we were in Istrago. The festival was outside, next to the church, which was the center of most activity in town. A woman from the English family told us that previous priests wouldn't let her and her husband take communion because they were divorced, but the new and younger priest welcomed their participation.

After a rest in Istrago, we drove north over the Brenner Pass to Innsbruck, where we boarded one of the excellent trains in that area. We traveled to St. Gallen, Switzerland, about four hours away. Everything was green, clean, and mountains and valleys whizzed by in a picturesque blend. At five o'clock, at our hotel, a note from Moraga neighbors said they would meet us at six. We met our longtime friends, sat at an outdoor cafe for beer and conversation. Tom went back to the room for our camera. When he returned, he had a two-page fax that came from Tony, birthday greetings to his dad, who turned 57 that day. It would be his last birthday.

The friends we were with that day, now in 2022, are no longer friends because of politics, something we didn't even talk about most of the years we were neighbors. Raising children, growing flowers, learning how to write, we were busy with the moving parts of our lives.

Venice, where we visited next, was full of pigeon droppings and tourists. One hundred thousand tourists arrive each day at that time of year. No count on the pigeons. Everything needed a coat of paint...and more. The look was referred to as "elegant decay."

My favorite thing in Venice was hanging out in St. Mark's Square in the evening. At least four outdoor cafes had bands that played. You could stroll from one to another and listen, clapping appreciatively. The music from "Cats" was popular. If you sat down, you paid a premium. We paid $20 to $25 for two beers, but for that you get to sit in this enormous, historic square, which Napoleon conquered and called the "greatest drawing room in the world."

This is one of the experiences that made me feel like a cosmopolitan citizen of the world. I unconsciously compared the United States to the countries I visited.

In Rome, we saw the great sites: the Forum; the Colosseum; fountains, piazzas. No documentation, the guide said, of Christians being killed in the Coliseum. Other places, yes, but not there. On to the Vatican, St. Peters and the museums. Without Cellini and Michelangelo, where would Rome be?

Then, we saw the lights of Naples and soon the skyline of Palermo, eyeing both cities at their best. The dirt, the grit, and the grime invisible from the ferry where we were surrounded by the blue ocean. We had been warned many times to be careful. Best to carry anything of value under your clothes, like a purse or billfold.

We walked a thin edge near disaster that whole trip. Maybe all our lives.

Our tour of Palermo, on the island of Sicily, included the main church, the Imperial Palace—where guards were everywhere—and other beautiful buildings, but what we saw was the scruffy streets, the beggars, the traffic—worse, if possible, than Rome. The local guide said they paid high taxes and got no services. Every American was interested, so the guide explained the history of the Mafia: for hundreds of years the Spaniards, and other invaders, ruled but offered the citizens no protection, thus the citizenry took over that function. That was the beginning of the Mafia. Not until this century, with the introduction of drugs, did it become what we know it as today.

We arrived in Agrigento and went to the Valley of the Temples. Seven temples in various stages of restoration, eight miles of wall, all from the 5th or 6th century BCE. Three hundred thousand people lived there, with 150,000 slaves doing the work.

Across the Straits of Messina, we arrived in the "toe" of the boot that is Italy with 400 miles to cover that day, much of it along the ancient Appian Way. Through mountains and countless fields.

Tom had been in Sorrento 35 years before. Built on the side of a steep hill of white rock, many of the buildings seemed to grow right out of the cliffs. White rock, lush vegetation, and tourists abound.

On Capri, we wanted to go to the Blue Grotto—something Tom had wanted to do all those years ago, but it had been closed back then. As we listened to the description of the boat tour, then got into a smaller boat to wait for access, Tom decided he wasn't up to it.

Back in Istrago once more.

"The best latte anywhere," we told them at the café, "the best spaghetti." Two doors from us. No menu. Carla tried to describe turkey, but didn't know the word, so she said, "Bigger than a chicken."

"Gobble, gobble," Tom said. She laughed.

Tired, not feeling well, Tom didn't stay for dinner.

I finished dinner alone. Carla paid special attention to me. I ordered two lattes and Bailey's Irish Cream and invited Carla to join me.

I told her about Tom. "He is sick. He probably will not get well. Now, my friend's husband has the same sickness."

We cried together.

The next morning, we had a farewell coffee at Carla's. She gave us a box to "open later" and a small package. The box contained two wine glasses from her restaurant and a good luck charm.

Thank you, my friend. I'm afraid it will take more than that!

Then it was on to France. There, the past was so present: the Roman Empire that spread north and west, building columns, coliseums, cities, a culture of which much still exists today.

"The Roman baths of 2000 years ago are better than the Italian showers of today," Tom commented.

Arles has a coliseum, built by the Romans, which is less decayed than the one in Rome. Bull fights are still held there. An ancient theater. The city replete with the leavings of the Romans.

I was looking forward to going home more than Tom was. He faced chemotherapy again and his energy was low. He often slept fifteen or more hours a day. Where else could he go after this escape?

I offered to cut our trip short and go home sooner, but he didn't want to. He could sleep there as well as anywhere, maybe better than at home, with our uninvited guest now muscling into every cupboard and drawer. Couldn't you leave us any space? Did you have to dominate every square inch?

Paris on a gray day looked wintry. Not all the leaves were gone, but I noted the black outline of many bare trees. An appropriate day to visit "La Cité" the place where the city began on the island that holds Notre Dame.

I left Tom at the hotel and walked. At the Île de la Cité, where Notre Dame is located, I bought one ticket for the prison and the Sainte-Chapelle, saw several documents signed by Robespierre, and visited the prison cell of Marie Antoinette.

The small Sainte-Chapelle has stained glass windows on every wall and is beautiful even on a gray day. On a bright day, it must be smashing.

History bore down on me there. The heaviness of events lingered in the air.

******

We returned from Europe in November of 1993. In the bank one day, we ran into a friend. She looked at Tom and shock spread across her face. He had lost weight and looked gaunt and tired.

In the new year, his decline continued. He wasn't strong enough for chemo, and in spite of blood transfusions, his body was losing platelets at a rapid rate.

"If he so much as scratches himself and it bleeds, take him to emergency," the doctor said. Tom was in and out of the hospital, with little energy even to do the most basic things. The doctor decided the pancreas was the reason Tom didn't retain platelets, so he began talking about surgery.

In February, I called the doctor and asked how long he thought Tom had to live.

"Four to six months," he replied, "unless we can turn things around."

These last months of his life were awful. The uninvited guest marched through our house as if he were the true owner, denying us any comfort or solace. No, you can't sit there!

By April, I didn't think he was strong enough for surgery, but there seemed to be no alternative. He said, go ahead, so in early May, we did. After surgery, he got an infection. The bags of medication they used to treat the infection were black, denoting how toxic the illness was.

On Thursday night, I stayed in the hospital, on a cot in his room, but got little sleep. Once, at about 4 a.m. Tom was awake, feeling terrible. I held him. We both cried. The nurse came in, held us both, and cried as well.

The last time I held him or he held me. I'm glad I was there, to hold him, to cry with him. I remember the last time we made love. It was in those awful last months, and it wasn't vigorous. After, I lay in bed and cried, knowing it possibly could have been the last time.

On Friday morning, after surgery and the infection, he was taken to ICU. They got my permission to put a respirator in his throat, telling me we could still communicate with him, but we really couldn't. Tony and Carrie canceled a trip they had planned for that weekend. Phil arrived from Santa Barbara.

Sunday. We left the hospital. Phil went to the store and bought every kind of sweet junk food. Ding Dongs. Oreos. I don't know why.

The last thing I heard Tom say, and he repeated it over and over, was "Love, luv, love."

Monday afternoon, I watched him take his last breath, finally finished with the pain.

I walked out of the hospital carrying his shoes, thinking how strange. He came in wearing them. This is all that is left of the living body, the person who entered through the front door.

At his service, I had "Amazing Grace" played on bagpipes. One of my friends, who knew I wasn't a believer, said, "Why did you have that song played?" I couldn't answer her, except to say that it touches me.

Chapter Seventeen

Faith in my Own Experiences:
Since Feeling Comes First

I am a different person than the one you met in the early chapters. Though I've thought about religion a great deal, I'm not a theologian. When I think about why I changed as I did from a Christian girl to a nonbeliever, the words of e.e. cummings come to mind:

since feeling is first,
who pays any attention
to the syntax of things
will never wholly kiss you...

Feelings come first for me.

Do feelings come from the gut? I'm not sure, but we know the phrase "gut feeling," and have probably said, "I just have a feeling," about something or other. When we meet people, sometimes we instinctively like or dislike them. Instinct probably plays a part in many choices we make.

When I started living on my own, I went in the direction of people and situations that felt good to me. My longtime friend, Jackie, is someone I just liked. When I was about 20, I applied for a stewardess (as they were called then) job. I flew to Seattle and was offered the position but decided against it. I'm not sure why, except I had a feeling that I shouldn't do it. Jackie agreed with my choice.

Just out of the family "nest," I didn't go to church regularly, though I wasn't yet ready to think about leaving the faith. Not at all. Lots of things had to happen. I had to witness differences within the church. I had to read. I had to question. I had miles to go before I slept.

The first steps, really, go back to when my family changed churches, and I'd been told I didn't need to worry about hell. What a relief! (And how quickly I bought into that idea.) Or, even before that, when I observed the differences in belief from one Christian church to another.

In more recent times, many Christian churches don't put so much emphasis on hell, but talk instead of "original sin," as in, we are born imperfect, subject to various instincts, some of which can lead to unhealthy or unhappy living, so we need a savior to help us do the right thing. Christianity has had a beneficent influence on many people's lives, so I don't have any problem with those who choose to stay in the church. My experience, my truth, leaves me responsible for being a good person on my own.

By the time I was a young woman, the beliefs from the Nazarene Church were not foremost in my thinking. The Kingdom beliefs were. That's where I started as a young person. I worked. When I wasn't working, I wanted to spend time with my friends and have fun. I didn't consciously reject those beliefs, but, increasingly, my time went toward other things.

I understand why people who have strict beliefs, whether they be Christian, Muslim or something else, try to keep their children away from the world in general—from people who don't believe as they do, who do things they think are wrong. The children might be attracted to those things, as I was.

With both churches, it seemed like everything that was fun or exciting was off limits. Or, perhaps, it was just that other things were seen as trivial by comparison to what you could be doing for the Lord.

Throughout my life, quite a few people have told me of having personal encounters with God or some other supernatural being. I don't question their experience, or that it might have a major impact on their lives, but that hasn't happened to me. So, most of the rewards I might have gotten from doing holy work were way off in some almost unimaginable future.

Two subjects dominated the Kingdom church preachings: first, we were the chosen people; second, Jews, through diabolical means, controlled most institutions. We were taught that they were the "synagogue of satan."

Over time, I questioned the divine origins of the Bible and eventually believed that the Bible was written by men, not God. These men may have believed they were inspired by God, but the biggest reason I eventually lost faith in the Bible is that it's written from a male point of view. Now, perhaps, over time, that is due to the ways men chose to interpret scripture. However, in major religions that take the Bible as the holy book, men dominate, and domination means ruling over someone else. Women are told what to wear, what to do, what they can and can't do in dozens of countries around the world. Even in the United States—a bastion of freedom for some, especially white males—many men think it is their right to dominate women. And many women agree or go along with it. That was true in both the first and the second church I was taken to as a child.

I just can't believe patriarchy is the way things should be. Women have had to fight for their rights for centuries. I simply can't support anything that is patriarchal, though getting away from it entirely is just about impossible.

I'm not anti-male. I raised two boys and know many men who don't believe in the patriarchy. But it is a dominant system and has been for centuries, so it's hard to get rid of. Many women support a patriarchal system or are so accustomed to it they can't see life another way.

As to the belief about Jews controlling government, finances, etc., I've seen little evidence for that. Henry Ford, who owned the *Dearborn Independent,* published many antisemitic articles. In particular, he republished the *Protocols of the Elders of Zion.* According to the website, pbs.org, "The *Protocols of the Elders of Zion* was a notorious forgery that originally came from Russia and was translated into English. It claimed the existence of an international Jewish conspiracy—that a group of Jews got together and basically planned the fate of the world, be it financial catastrophe, be it war. The world was controlled by this little cabal of Jews. This forgery was printed in *The Dearborn Independent* as a factual piece. So someone reading it would take this to be the news."

My brother told me it was the Ashkenazi Jews who were the bad ones, but I know of no evidence for that, either. I came to know several Ashkenazis who were good people. I had no reason to suspect them of anything of a bad nature.

As I've mentioned earlier, I cannot see the righteousness in taking this land from the native people and enslaving others to do the heavy lifting of building a new country. Certainly, virtue exists in the United States Constitution, but it, like other documents, was written by men and it isn't perfect.

Leaving the Faith of Our Fathers

******

After Tom died, trying to find my way, I took a trip to Idaho. My ties there have always been strong, family ties, memories. I went to the cemetery where so many relatives were buried.

The caretaker came out of his small, hot shed of an office at the rear of the cemetery as I approached, squinting in my direction. I gave him the name. He scratched his head and went back inside. Turning pages that crackled with the dry heat, he found "Ernest Young" and directed me down the middle road and a few rows to the right.

Father's grave is unmarked except for a small, rough piece of white metal with his name on it. An uncle gave us the plot, which lies near where other family members are buried. I wandered among the stones, reading names, remembering people.

Wiping sweat from my face, I felt it trickle between my breasts as I stood in the shade of a large and spreading tree. What is this place and what do these people have to do with me? Something brought me back here; some bond with my father that I can't express. I never knew his parents except through stories passed down. The uncles and aunts I've known. Aunt Lucy and Blanche, their warmth, liveliness, and joy still reside in me. They climbed ladders and picked peaches when they were in their nineties. I am determined to be like them, trampling across the earth, learning, loving, expounding, and experiencing all that is within my grasp.

"The women in my family have always been independent and have lived long lives," I say to myself. "I will, too." I whisper it again.

Here, I gather material from the circle of where and who I came from, what happened before and to me. The Idaho farm country is drawn in my brain, as are the people. Until my synapses fail and my system shuts down, these people, this place will be with me.

With Tom's death, I think about the others who have passed. It is hard to leave this silent place, with the echoes of voices, faces, and events from a faraway time.

"I want to buy a stone for Dad's grave," I told Mother, after driving the few miles from the cemetery to the outskirts of Nampa, to the property where she still lived and I grew up, though in a different house. I have no idea why I wanted to do this, what connection it had to Tom's death, or to me. I never liked my father. Why would I? He was old, mean, and disappointing as a parent. I was young and hopeful, yearning for brightness, life, excitement. Still, he gave me life. Maybe buying him a stone was a way of forgiving him.

While there, I talk with my family and his family—Tom's aunts and brother, connecting where possible.

Someone asked me if I would move back to Idaho. Tom is gone. My sons are on their own. I never considered it.

I walked the banks of the Boise River. In my room at night, I mulled and stretched and pulled at thoughts and feelings, needing to coalesce myself.

Then I returned the rental car and boarded the plane. I was going home. To California.

******

Two lives, my father's and my husband's, were not the only important influences in my life, but they were pivotal. My father, with his demands for absolute obedience, along with the church's emphasis on sin and damnation, and the school's authoritarian ways, all were part of a patriarchal system that did nothing to foster my independence, self-confidence, or intellectual pursuits. At sixty, I still had traces of the feelings of inferiority that came from this childhood.

My husband was not as oppressive. Still, he saw me in the traditional role of wife and mother. Though I fulfilled those roles, when I began to step beyond them—to go to school and to question the role of women and the role of men—he became frustrated. If he was playing the role of breadwinner, then I should be playing the part that he had for me in his head.

Winning his approval was next to impossible. If he thought I behaved badly, he became silent, sometimes for days. It took many years and required marriage counseling to understand that his silence was a power he held over me, making me wretched as long as I allowed it. I was advised to ask what the problem was, offer to talk about it and try to solve it, but if he refused to talk, my responsibility was over. I could go on with my life. Once I did that and stopped being upset by his silence, it didn't work for him anymore.

"You look nice, dear," was the most he ever said, no matter how much I tried to be thin and look good. It was the same thing that he said to his mother.

We shared some wonderful things, particularly the lives of our two sons. We laughed and loved each other. We experienced things together that no one else will ever know.

He was a handsome man who had been president of his college fraternity. Many such men would not look at a woman who was merely a high school graduate. He provided financial stability that made it possible for me to take classes, get a bachelor's and master's degree, volunteer, and move away from his image of what I should be.

When I encounter someone who tells me absolutely what to do and how to do it, I react, overreact, really, determined not to be led in that way.

Both men may still have an influence on the way I react to other men.

For the rest of my life...what is possible? What can I be on my own? I have traveled too far, on my own, to go back now. Tracings of the nice little girl, whom larger people smile down on, are still in me, shadows of wanting approval, but I will step out of that shadow.

Connecting to my past, I begin reaching for a long-ago history, somewhere in the murky mud of the collective unconscious.

Many stories whirl around me and run through my body. I must find a map for the rest of my journey, or maybe allow it free form, or just step a little ahead, as far as I can see through the mist. Some faith is required, not in a greater being, but in myself.

After Tom's death, old friends, Jackie and Mary, from our before-marriage apartment days visit. For a week, we talk, catching up on all the things we didn't have time for in the midst of child rearing, and tending to all necessary duties. We drive up the coast to Mendocino, chattering about how it was all those years ago and how we are now, laughing hysterically, listening somberly, renewing and strengthening our bonds, like restoring the threads of an old coat.

Mother and I take a cruise to Alaska. We meet in Seattle. I see a frail woman in a wheelchair, and reluctantly, sadly, recognize my mother. We travel north to Vancouver in a motor coach, with other Idahoans from Nampa and Caldwell, that Mother knew. We arrive at the ship.

A wheelchair is in place to carry Mother aboard. We unpack and go on deck to watch the ship sail smoothly out of port, under the Lions' Gate Bridge, past Stanley Park— "remember when we were there"—and out to sea.

Later that evening, Mother turns to me: "When do we leave?"

Once I get home, I quickly, get the pictures from the voyage developed, send them to Idaho in an album so Mother can show visiting relatives, so the reality of the trip will not be lost in that mind where faces, facts, and incidents drop over the edge into some vast cavernous area and cannot be retrieved.

******

I started writing again, now working on a novel. It's my way to the truth, an expression that satisfies me as nothing else does. It gives me peace and joy. Whether others see the words or not, the first pleasure is in creating them.

Almost exactly two years after Tom's death, I fly to Frankfurt, bicycle from Vienna to Budapest, then fly to Oslo, traversing the Scandinavian countries of Tom's roots. In a Stockholm hotel, I rip pages of his surname—and mine—from the telephone book, with the old-world spelling, to take back to the children.

While Tom was sick, my sister visited. After his death, she comes again. We drive the highways of California, visit cousins, enjoy family reunions and each other.

"I preach to everyone but Lois," she explained one time. Traveling to Oklahoma, Canada, Spokane and England, she speaks to believers and those who will listen. She never marries, choosing to give her life to the Lord.

On one visit, she reads my political columns. Pointing to one on abortion and one on gun control, she says, "Of course, I don't agree with these."

"I know." After a pause, "When is your next trip?"

"Oklahoma. Next month."

"Where will you speak?"

"At the church in Tulsa... Do you remember when we were in Dallas? There was a woman wearing a large hat who was very nice to us?"

"Yeah, well sort of. It's been a long time."

"Well, anyway, she lives in Dallas with her daughter now. She still asks about you."

"That's nice."

Sometimes we fall silent, recognizing the limits even as we acknowledge how much we share. What binds us is beyond definition.

We have a family gathering at Mother's house, a place where the past hangs out and around: the hutch with dishes, each with its own tale to tell; the English tea cups bought in Victoria, wrapped carefully in layers of paper, carried home, shown to everyone and then set on a shelf; the round oak table on a heavy pedestal that spreads to clawed feet; here we sat as children. Photographs of our dead, together, in permanent clothes, on the wall. My sister and brothers, too, have been touched by painful experiences in their lives.

Harry is not of this world, but the one he believes in, one in which an all-knowing, all-powerful God rules, where everyone lives in sufficiency, order, peace, and fairness. The lion rests with the lamb, and nothing makes them afraid. Even what we want at the end is not so different, but I see no divinity to make it possible.

We are joined by another brother, Stan. He does not like this world either, agreeing with Harry and Ernie and our mother, but he finds it more difficult to avoid contentious relationships with some of his children and several divorces.

His voice often has our father's bitter edge. This has not made his life easy, the quarrelling, having rolled over and over, stayed active. The lines of his face, the creases along the cheeks are deep now.

Together, we sit, for a brief time, remember, share, laugh at our past as if it were a comedy we had seen together. Soon, we will go separate ways, believe and act differently. But this laughter, this brief touching, will be carried with us, stored in a secure chamber near the heart.

Chapter Eighteen

The Rest

Sometimes, but rarely, in writing, you hit something, a nerve, a memory jog, a coalescing of thought and feeling. You sit upright, look outside, shudder with feeling. You've discovered a rich vein, a piece of your being, a kind of epiphany. That piece makes you whole in the moment.

Writing filled my need for self-expression and helped make sense of my life. I'd studied poetry, which often flowed into prose. The Surrealists influenced me to go in whatever direction I needed to and not to worry about the form.

I still marvel at how much freedom came with the Surrealist ideas. I was always inclined to jump from here to there in writing and speaking. Once, when Tom heard me do that, he asked me how I got from talking about my mother to the donut shop. I thought about it and described the trail, though I usually didn't need all the steppingstones. It happened naturally and, when allowed and supported, this ability could take me to exciting places.

I don't know how I could have stayed in the church and expressed myself fully. I'm thinking here of the two churches I went to as a child, where there are too many restrictions on what you can read, write, or feel.

After I left Christianity, I read, thought about, even experimented a bit with other religions. Buddhism, for example, but it seems to have another method of inducing guilt—making all desires undesirable—which drove me away. Now maybe that's an incorrect interpretation of Buddhism. I didn't study it in depth, but after a few months I dropped my attendance at the local sangha and stopped reading about it. The Baha'i faith has some interesting aspects, but I haven't pursued it. I liked the Unitarian Church I attended a few times, but I didn't (and don't) have a strong desire to get involved with any faith.

Writing was my one constant. I wrote columns for the League of Women Voters that came out weekly in the local paper. The newspaper put the League's column on the left side of the page. Opposite it on the right side was a column with a right wing bent. The man who wrote it called the women of the League lefties and Communists. Never had anything good to say about us! Once I met him and was seated next to him at dinner. He was gracious, never referring to the words he had thrown in my direction over the years.

I also wrote travel articles about the trips I took to Europe with Tom. I stopped writing for the LWV around the time Tom died, but, later, for the same paper, the Contra Costa Sun, I wrote a column called "Personally Speaking." I could say whatever I wanted! You may think that freedom would be great, and I liked it, but I discovered that everyone is a critic. Whether I said something they didn't like politically, or if I messed up on some minor detail, someone noticed and called me out. I continued with that column until 2000.

I began work on a novel that I published in 2000, called "Where Lilacs Bloom." It is political. The GOP becomes the GOD party and seeks to stifle free speech. A woman is imprisoned without a trial. I will leave it there.

It's very hard to get attention in the writing world these days, so the book got little notice. Easy to publish, but hard to get readers. Like most writers, I hate trying to sell my work. Writing, I love!

Travel continued as a lively interest. When I traveled with Tom, we usually weren't part of a group, though we'd sign up for a tour of whatever town we were in that lasted a couple of hours. We drove on our own, made our own hotel reservations. After he died, I took several bicycle trips with friends in Europe, an excellent way to see the countries without being part of a crowd. This on-the-ground trip gave me a good feel for the culture and the people.

In Hungary the school children would stop their play to say "hallo" as we rode past. The cars gave us a wide space, which someone told us was good because many don't have brakes. So many things one hears along the way, some true, some local legend.

In the Spring of 1998, Mother fell. My siblings called me, and I flew up that same day. Mother's dementia was quite severe by that time. She knew her children that lived nearby better than she knew me, as she didn't see me as often. She thought I was her sister.

We took her to the hospital and, from there, we found a nursing facility for her to stay in. My brothers wanted us to bring her home. They thought the care was up to the women in the family; however, Mother was physically larger than any of us and we weren't able to take care of her 24 hours a day. Though they acquiesced and paid some of the cost, it wasn't what they preferred. A severe mistrust of the medical field stays with them to this day, as well as a feeling that she should die at home with her family caring for her.

I went to Idaho and visited her while she was at the care facility. The last time I saw her eat, she was doing what patients typically do at that stage of dementia: "pocketing" her food, that is putting it in her mouth and then forgetting to swallow it. She didn't know the difference between the food and the paper napkin. I hated seeing her like that.

A few days later, I was in Germany with friends, John and Jackie, when I got the call from Tony. Mother passed.

I remember trying to connect with this woman, my mother, in her late life. "I'm Lois, your daughter," I said. A few feet apart, we looked at each other. We could touch each other, but she who bore me, couldn't find the synapses that held our bond. It's a kind of death.

And even though our connection was frayed in her last days, I still—25 years later—carry her words, her influence. She comes to me in dreams. So does Tom. Sometimes they are together.

I flew to Boise with Tony and his wife and baby for the memorial service. Once again, I heard the promises of resurrection and a kingdom on earth.

Our younger brother, Larry, had always lived with Mother. He had jobs but never managed to be fully independent, and his problem was not diagnosed. So, when Mother died, her assets—basically the property she owned—was to go to caring for Larry. My sister had the direct responsibility for watching out for him.

In many ways, this brought me and my siblings closer together, at least initially, but we didn't agree on how to handle Larry. My other brothers were sterner in their approach than my sister and I were, and this disagreement never went away.

I said, "Well, we'll go to every government agency around and see what help we can get." None of them would have said that! We found a job for him. He was picked up in a van, driven to Boise with several other people. They did janitorial service in some of the government buildings there. He lived for a time in a mobile home and then moved into a small apartment in the same house where my sister lived.

I wrote for various online sites, such as Patch.com—"Caffeine Chronicles"—eventually got acquainted with poets in town and was the Poet Laureate of Benicia from 2012 to 2014. At this same time, I helped found Benicia Literary Arts and, following that, with others, I founded Carquinez Village, an organization for older people, part of a network of "villages" across the country that support, inform, and provide services to older people.

In the Spring of 2012, I attended the wedding of a grandnephew in Idaho. While there, my sister, younger brother, and I went to McCall to have lunch at Shore Lodge, something we've done throughout our lives. We were celebrating Larry's birthday. The next day, we watched him bowl and met his friends there. It would be the last time I saw him.

I got a call one morning in July. Larry had died of a heart attack. Another quick trip to Idaho. Another time of sharing grief and the teachings of the church.

Grieving for Larry included the sadness that his life had been limited. He had always wanted to marry but would see a picture of a beautiful woman he didn't even know and decide that she was the one he wanted. Little reason went into his choices, little practical thinking. In his last years, he hung out with a woman who rode the van to work with him.

Of course, he went to the Kingdom church all his life. He had limited mental capacity, so I don't know how he understood all he was told, though I saw him fearful at times.

Once when he was working on the janitorial job, he was worried. They were going to have a Halloween party. Though we'd had fun with Halloween as kids, by the early 2000s, it was seen as evil by some of my family.

"I don't want to go. It's devil worship," he said to me.

"Don't go, then. It's a party. You don't have to go." I responded, though I could hear from his tone that he wanted to go, but also didn't want to go to what the church people would see as ungodly.

After my generation, some of my nieces and nephews, and their children, were far stricter about things like that than we had been. The patriarchy was stronger, though possibly more benevolent than in my father's day. The church in Oregon where one of my brothers and his family attended trained girls in how to be subservient mothers, dutiful, hard-working, obedient.

No! I hated seeing girls taught to be subservient! It comes from my gut, from some instinct the preachers couldn't reach, from my own being as a woman.

Just as the hymns we grew up with repeated the phrases about our being weak and frail, so needy of a (male) savior, females were trained to stay at home and be mothers. I did that, too, but I didn't stop there. I was never obedient!

My writings have reflected a strong belief in the strength of women. *Where Lilacs Bloom* has a female protagonist who solves problems her way. *Late Harvest Green*, another novel set in Idaho, has strong female characters. One can be strong without being obnoxious.

******

To celebrate my 70th birthday, my sons and spouses and grandchildren plus two friends hiked the Grand Canyon from the North Rim to the South Rim. My grandchildren were nine and eleven at the time. You just can't see the Canyon from the top like you can down inside. I feel a connection even now, having walked the fourteen miles down, not seeing many other hikers on that trail, staying two nights at Phantom Ranch near the Colorado River, with lots of games and laughter and resting, then hiking ten miles up Bright Angel Trail.

I've wanted to see and experience the world, not with a bucket list or a camera in front of my face all the time, but with open eyes, mind, and heart. Three weeks in New Zealand, another three in China, a tour with friends in India, and through most countries in Europe. In 2015, it was the Eastern European countries that drew me.

Before I traveled anywhere, what I'd heard since I was very young was that our country, America, the United States, was the greatest country on earth. I now have a more nuanced view of that. I admire the objectives our Constitution and Declaration of Independence laid out, but learning that those freedoms were only granted to white men with property, that Blacks were counted as three-fifths of a person, that the price paid by Native Americans and Blacks was enormous and that the results of this discrimination have lasting impacts on millions to this day—well, that requires that I acknowledge all the history, not just the parts I like.

Still, had Trump not come on the scene, I probably wouldn't have written this book. It was in 2015, when I took a trip to Idaho. With my sister, a cousin, and my long-time friend, Jackie, we drove north from Boise and stayed in a hotel near Cascade.

Over breakfast, I said something about Trump, not positive, as you could guess.

"Oh, you've got it all wrong," my friend said. "He's generous—that just doesn't make the news—everyone at our church likes him."

My sister or cousin didn't say anything. I left breakfast early, suddenly feeling alone. Christians who couldn't admire Barack Obama now give their hearts to DT! Since then, I've shaken my head repeatedly and have lost a measure of respect for these people that are close to me, women who I've felt always lived true Christian lives—being caring, kind, understanding, and loving to others—now falling into that camp that loves DT and see those of us who don't as somehow, wrong, or bad, or sinful.

Until this time, maybe a part of me felt I'd abandoned the church just so I could be more self-indulgent, do what I wanted. But I don't cede the moral high ground after these recent years.

In 2021, I was in Colorado at my son's home when I got the news that my oldest brother, Harry, had died. He was always kind to me, never asked why I was the way I was. Startling, his death, though we hadn't spent much time together in many years. At weddings, however, usually one of his grandkids getting married, at the receptions, as people mixed and mingled, usually the four of us siblings end up sitting together, finding a bond, an unspoken comfort just sitting there together. So natural.

It's the summer of 2022. My siblings reside in Idaho. I visit them in March when Steve, a nephew, dies. As always, we are cordial. I still feel the bond created so long ago, but I feel little will change between us. They believe absolutely that they are right. End of story.

"The Bike Trail," a poem I've been writing and rewriting for years, expresses who I am and what my expectations are for after this life. It ends like this:

Leaving the Faith of Our Fathers

When I am gone
        the bike trail
        will not look different
        the seasons will continue

I would like to return
  in wind & cloud
   swing through oak trees
  go at that speed

        you have transformed
these words into something
            of your own
              a life   I never knew
              a home with a hall
              through which I will never
           pass

my words will go
          where I cannot & will report
         my thoughts
         when they are
       no more

I will
   be
   my
   words
     influence
     echoes

I move forward with an everlasting desire to learn more, to laugh, and be grateful for the good life that I've had, and for daily joy.

Epilogue

My Conclusions

As you realize by now, I didn't suddenly turn around one day and change all my beliefs. It was a process of reading, listening, traveling, and living, of trusting my own experiences and instincts.

I recently read the "Ten Commitments" written by the American Humanist Association's Center for Education. I guess I'm now a Humanist, because I agree with all their commitments.

In my own words, we should treat everyone fairly and honestly, and with kindness and respect. I respect your right to believe in whatever you choose. I expect the same from you.

To enable this in society, the separation of church and state is essential. Witness the countries in the world where these two institutions are brought together—Iran and Afghanistan—as well as others. When religion is forced upon everyone, it makes for an unjust society.

I feel that laws can't be equal when they are enforced on women but not men. In that regard, since no laws restrict males and their expression of their sexuality, women also should have full autonomy over their own bodies. If you don't believe in abortion, don't have one, but don't pass judgment on others.

I've made the point about patriarchy. As a child, the preacher, the school principal, the police, and my father all were important control figures, and all were male. I've reacted to that and have been an advocate for women throughout my life. I raised two sons. I think they are fine with that.

I've come to feel that as a society, we need to acknowledge the collective sins of the past and make amends in ways that are reasonable and helpful to the current generations who are their progeny. Blacks brought here as slaves and Native Americans were treated horrendously in our history. Many still are to this day. Recognizing the wrongs we have done—as individuals or as a society—is a healthy process.

I respect the place we live and for all living creatures that share the Earth as home.

I'm still learning—by listening, reading, and experiencing life. I hope you are, too!

The End

Acknowledgements

Many people helped with this publication. I've been
working with Benicia Literary Arts (benicialiteraryarts.org) for
many years. I taught a memoir class there and from the class, a
memoir writing group developed. The group has met twice a
month for over ten years. *Leaving the Faith of our Fathers* was
edited by those writers, which include Mary Eichbauer, Linda
Hastings, Tamar Enoch, and the late Carolyn Plath. Their
encouragement was essential to finishing the book.

The book club I've been a part of for thirty years is another
group of smart, kind, and caring women. This group includes
Anne Grodin, Melinda Kavanagh, Gail Murray, Loella
Haskew, Linda Hastings, Dixie Mohan, Kate Kingsley, Harriet
Murphy, and Lois Kazakoff.

Finally, the Ladies Lunch Bunch has been having lunch
and more for over thirty years. We encourage, support, and
help each other grow, laughing and crying as we live through
what life throws at us. They are Laurie Sizemore, Anne Grodin,
Karen Strachan, Gayle Vasser, and the late Charmian Dobell
who was with us for many years.

The front cover is a painting by Samantha McNally. Carrie
Requist, my daughter-in-law, designed the covers. The rest of

my family always have my back. That includes my sons, Tony and Phil, my granddaughter, Melissa Requist and her husband, Alex Bixel, my grandson, Wren Requist and his wife, Kate Brown Requist, and my granddaughter, Olivia Requist.

When I moved from one town to another in the San Francisco Bay Area—Moraga to Benicia—some people thought I was stepping down. I've been here 25 years now, living in the downtown area where I walk every day. I'm fortunate to have such a good life and a supportive community.

www.ingramcontent.com/pod-product-compliance
Lightning Source LLC
Chambersburg PA
CBHW071512140726
47997CB00005B/1946